Air France at 90

France's Largest Airline

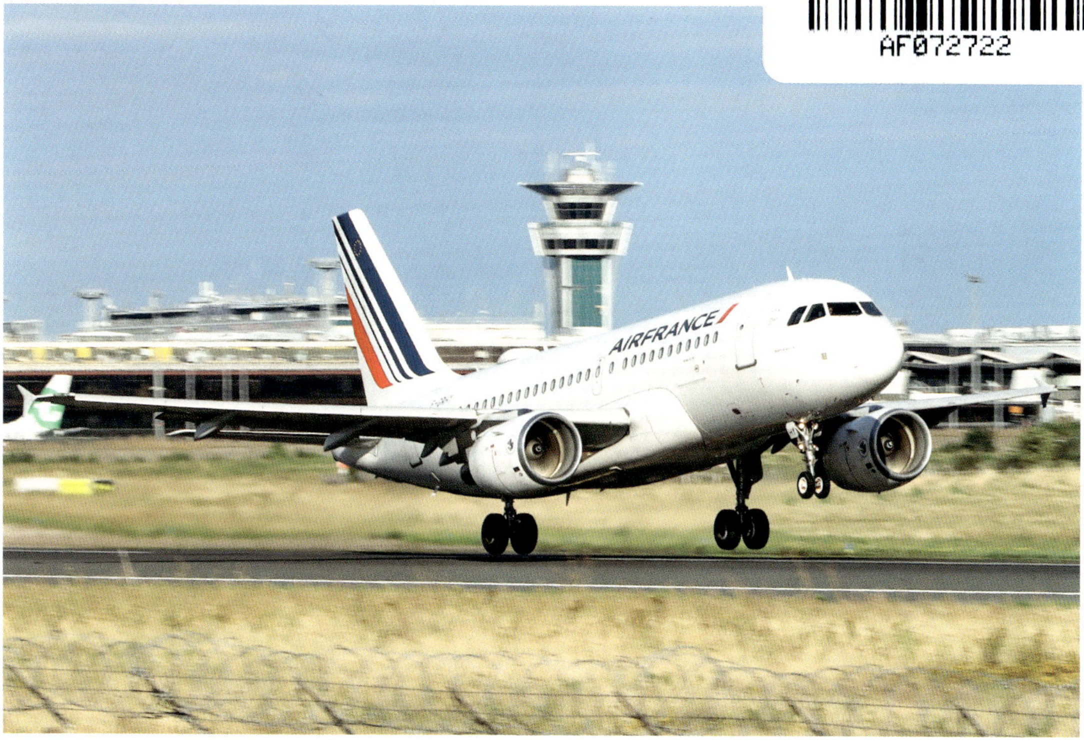

BABAK TAGHVAEE

KEY Books

AIRLINES SERIES, VOLUME 18

Front cover image: F-GSQU is one of Air France's 43 Boeing 777-328ERs. Together with 18 Boeing 777-228ERs, they form the backbone of the wide-body passenger aircraft fleet. On 25 September 2023, the Air France-KLM Group announced plans to place an order for 50 Airbus A350-900 and A350-1000 aircraft, with purchase rights for 40 additional aircraft. Deliveries are expected in 2026 through to 2030. The A350-1000s will take the place of Air France's Boeing 777-328ER. (Babak Taghvaee)

Title page image: F-GRHY, with construction number (c/n) 1616, is an Airbus A319-111s in service with Air France. The aircraft is taking off from Paris-Orly (flight number AF7572) to Calvi on 20 August 2023. In that month, Air France had 14 airworthy A319-111s, which were mainly used for short- and medium-range flights. (Babak Taghvaee)

Contents page image: Two of Air France's Airbus A220-300s. F-HZUO returning from Warsaw (flight AF1147) is on 26L runway at Charles de Gaulle Airport, while F-HZUB takes off from runway 26R for Porto (flight AF1528) on 9 August 2023. By the end of 2025, Air France will have 60 A220-300 single-aisle and narrow-body airliners in use, replacing its A318s, A319s and some of its A320s. (Babak Taghvaee)

Back cover image: Airbus A380-861 prior to delivery and still wearing its temporary factory code. This airline began commercial service in August 2010 and was withdrawn from service in February 2022 almost two years after it had been put into storage. It was later scrapped at Tarbes. (EZ/ZX Collection)

Published by Key Books
An imprint of Key Publishing Ltd
PO Box 100
Stamford
Lincs PE9 1XQ

www.keypublishing.com

The right of Babak Taghvaee to be identified as the author of this book has been asserted in accordance with the Copyright, Designs and Patents Act 1988 Sections 77 and 78.

Copyright © Babak Taghvaee, 2023

ISBN 978 1 80282 831 3

All rights reserved. Reproduction in whole or in part in any form whatsoever or by any means is strictly prohibited without the prior permission of the Publisher.

Typeset by SJmagic DESIGN SERVICES, India.

Contents

Introduction 4

Chapter 1 The Narrow-Body Fleet 13

Chapter 2 The Wide-Body Fleet 44

Chapter 3 The Regional Jets Fleet 78

Appendix 1 Incidents and Accidents..84

Appendix 2 Air France Fleet Details as of August 2023 91

Introduction

On 7 October 2023, Air France celebrated its 90th anniversary. It has a fleet of 211 aircraft comprising 102 narrow-body and single-aisle passenger aircraft and 107 wide-body and long-haul examples, as well as two cargo aircraft. Its subsidiary, Air France Hop has 33 regional jets. Air France's aircraft fly to 191 destinations in 89 countries including 106 destinations and 66 seasonal routes in France and Europe. These aircraft collectively logged up to 835 flights per day in summer 2023.

In 2004, Air France acquired the Dutch airline KLM to create Air France-KLM Group. That year, a public exchange offer for KLM shares was launched by Air France, leading to the merger of these two companies and the birth of the Air France-KLM Group just a few months after privatisation of Air France in the same year. In a short period of time, the group became the world's largest airline operation in terms of turnover, and the third largest in terms of the number of passengers flown. It carried a staggering 66 million passengers on 550 aircraft in 2003. Four years after the merger of the two airlines and formation of the group, the aircraft transported 74 million passengers.

The group's global network has been co-ordinated around Air France's hub at Paris Charles de Gaulle Airport and Amsterdam-Schiphol Airport, two of the four biggest hubs in Europe. As of August 2023, Air France had 211 aircraft in its fleet and 43 more in its subsidiary, Air France Hop. KLM had 110 aircraft at its disposal while its subsidiary, KLM Cityhopper, had 64 aircraft.

In the past two decades, Air France has retired its four-engined wide-body passenger aircraft such as the Airbus A340s, A380s and Boeing 747-400 series and has replaced them with two-engine wide-body aircraft such as Boeing 777-328ERs and Airbus A350-941s. Those with two turbofan engines register less fuel consumption and reduced maintenance and operational costs, increasing the profitability of long-range flights for the airline. In addition, the fleet of narrow-body passenger aircraft has been modernised, with the replacement of the Airbus A318s and A319s with Airbus A220-300s.

In terms of revenue, Air France-KLM Group became the fifth largest airline group in January 2023. It had a revenue turnover of US$29.41bn and posted a profit of US$970m. The organisation has 78,950 staff and assets worth US$34bn.

Through its history, Air France has operated at least 932 passenger and cargo aircraft. In total, 211 are still in use. This book reviews the history and current status of the aircraft currently in use with Air France and the 33 passenger aircraft in use by its subsidiary airline, Air France Hop, as of August 2023.

Air France's History

The airline was formed on 30 August 1933 from a merger of five French airlines, Air Orient, Air Union, Compagnie Générale Aéropostale, Compagnie Internationale de Navigation Aérienne (CIDNA) and Société Générale des Transports Aériens (SGTA), the last named of which was the oldest commercial airline company of France. Over the course of seven years, the newly emerged Air France reduced the number of its aircraft from 259 to 90, mainly French, including Potez 62s, to reduce its maintenance and operational costs and increase its profitability.

The Potez 62, equipped with a pair of Gnome-Rhône 14Kirs Mistral Major piston engines, could carry 14 to 16 passengers across short-distance flights in France and to neighbouring countries, as well as in South America and the Far-East until 1940. At that point Air France's activities were gradually reduced following the occupation of northern France by Nazi Germany and then the free zone in 1942. During World War Two, the existing assets of the airline located outside the French mainland, particularly in North Africa, were used by 'Occupied Air France' or 'Free Air France', under the authority of General de Gaulle between 1940 and 1942, and then Lignes Aériennes Militaires (Military Air Lines) until 1945, when the war ended.

After World War Two, all of France's air transport companies were nationalised, including Air France, on 26 June 1945. On 29 December of the same year, Air France, which had resumed its operations after the war, was granted management of the entire French air transport network following a decree issued by the French government. The airline opened its first air terminal at Les Invalides in central Paris. Passengers checked in there before taking a coach to Le Bourget and later Orly airport to meet their flights. This service continued until 1961, when check-in was centralised at the airports. With its hub at Paris Le Bourget Airport, the airline established a network that covered 160,000km in 1946.

In 1946, the US-made Douglas DC-3 twin-engined passenger aircraft and DC-4 four-engined passenger aircraft entered service with Air France, taking the place of the last surviving tri-engined Dewoitine D.338s operated by the company and retired in 1945. In total, 83 variants of DC-3s were operated by Air France between 1946 and 1962 and 50 different DC-4s between 1946 and 1971.

In addition to the DC-4s, Air France operated many other piston-engined passenger aircraft for medium- and long-distance flights, including intercontinental and transoceanic models, before receiving its first jet-engine aircraft. They included two DC-6s (operated between 1949 and 1968), four Latécoère 631 flying boats (operated between 1949 and 1968), four Lockheed L-049s (operated between 1946 and 1950), 24 Lockheed L-749s (operated between 1947 and 1961), 24 L-1049s (operated between 1953 and 1968) and eight L-1649As (operated between 1957 and 1963).

France has also operated 16 different German-made Junkers Ju 52/3m tri-motors (1945–53), 49 different four-engined SNCASE SE.161 Languedocs (1945–52) and 12 double-decked and four-engined Bréguet 763 Deux-Ponts (1952–71) for passenger and freight transport in high demand, short- and medium-range flights, alongside the smaller DC-3s.

In 1959, Air France entered the jet age following delivery of its first Sud Aviation Caravelle medium-range, narrow-body jet airliners. Fifty were delivered to the airline, with the last of the type operating until 1981, when it was replaced with Boeing 727-228 Advanced aircraft. In same year, the airline began receiving Boeing 707 four-engined, long-range narrow-body airliners. In total, 41 different Boeing 707s were delivered over the following years replacing piston-engined Lockheed Constellation and Super Constellations. The Boeing variants comprised eight Boeing 707-320Bs and 12 Boeing 707-320Cs, which were ultimately replaced by wide-body Airbus A300s and A310s between 1982 and 1984.

Between 1968 and 1980, Air France received 29 Boeing 727-228 narrow-body jetliners to replace its Caravelles across medium-range flights, while 16 Boeing 747-128 wide-body passenger aircraft were delivered between 1970 and 1977. These replaced Boeing 707s for long-distance flights. In the years between 1974 and 1990, 23 Boeing 747-228s in three different variants, B (basic), BM (modernised) and F (freighter), were acquired. In addition to these, more Boeing 747-200 series were also leased by the airline in these years. During the 1990s, Boeing 747-400 series aircraft and two former Union De Transport Aerien (UTA) Boeing 747-3B3Ms replaced some of the ageing Boeing 747-228s.

While Boeing 747s connected France to long-distance destinations across all continents from 1970, six years later, the revolutionary Aérospatiale/BAC Concorde supersonic passenger aircraft almost halved flight times. Seven were delivered; one crashed in 2000 and six others remained in service until 2003, allowing customers who could afford the high fares, to fly between Paris and Washington Dulles or New York JFK in around four hours.

Air France also acquired a large number of classic Boeing 737 narrow-body jets including series 200 (24 aircraft between 1982 and 2002), series 300 (nine operated between 1991 and 2004), and series 500 (30 operated between 1990 and 2007), which were used for short- and medium-range flights mainly within Europe and France. They were eventually replaced by Airbus A320s between 1998 and 2006.

As of August 2023, Air France had 102 single-aisle passenger aircraft, comprising 29 A220s, six A318s, 14 A319s, 38 A320s and 15 A321s. The airline operated them for short- and medium-range flights, together with 13 ERJ170s and 20 ERJ190s, both regional jets operated by Air France Hop, mainly for flights within Europe, particularly inside France.

The airline also operates 107 wide-body and long-haul passenger aircraft. As of August 2023, these were 15 Airbus A330s, 21 A350s, 18 Boeing 777-228ERs, 43 Boeing 777-328ERs and ten Boeing 787-9s, which were used for long-range flights once served by the four-engined wide-body passenger aircraft such as Airbus A340s, A380s and the Boeing 747-400 series. In addition, Air France had a pair of Boeing 777-F28 wide-body aircraft for cargo transport.

A330s took the place of A300s and A310s between 1996 and 2002, while A350s replaced the A380s in 2020. Boeing 777-228ERs took the place of A340-200/300 series aircraft between 2005 and 2019, Boeing 777-328ERs took the place of Boeing 747s between 2005 and 2016 while Boeing 787-9s took the place of the last Airbus A340-300 series aircraft between 2016 and 2020.

Left: F-ANPG was the prototype Potez 62, which first flew on 28 January 1935. It was delivered to Air France on 10 April 1935 and was named *Albatros* in its service. (Havapeima's archive)

Below: This ex-French Air Force Douglas C-47A-1-DL is now privately owned. It has been painted as F-BBBE, a DC-3 that once served Air France in French overseas territories in the Indian Ocean between 1946 and 1966. (Babak Taghvaee)

F-BAZB (c/n 2073) was the second Lockheed L-049 Constellation to enter service with Air France. It first flew on 11 October 1946 and was delivered on 24 October 1946. It was later sold to TWA Transcontinental and Western Air on 11 January 1950. (Havapeima's archive)

France's second Boeing 707-328 narrow-body passenger aircraft with r/c F-BHSB (c/n 17614), in 1960. Equipped with four Pratt & Whitney JT4A turbojet engines enabled with Hush-Kits to reduce noise, the aircraft flew for the first time on 14 November 1959. It was delivered on 12 December 1959 and was first flown by Air France on 26 January 1960, receiving the *Château de Chambord* fleet name. Air France leased it to Cameron Airlines between December 1971 and June 1974. It remained in use by the airline until 12 November 1975 when it was broken-up at Paris-Orly Airport. (Havapeima's archive)

F-BOJB (c/n 19544) was the second of 29 Boeing 727-228 Advanced narrow-body passenger aircraft that Air France operated. It was delivered to Air France on 23 April 1968 and was in use until June 1986, when it was leased to Air Afrique. (Havapeima's archive)

F-BPVB (c/n 19750) was first flown on 7 March 1970, and is the airline's second Boeing 747-128, delivered on 25 March 1970. The aircraft remained in use with the airline until April 1995, when it was leased to Kabo Air. It was returned to Air France after four months and then broken up at Marseille-Marignane Airport. (Havapeima's archive)

This Boeing 747-128 with r/c F-BVPJ (c/n 2541) is the sole jumbo jet in Air France's stable and has been preserved. It was first flown on 26 October 1972, delivered to Air France on 21 February 1973 and put into service on 14 March 1973 under hire purchase. It remained there until 25 February 2000, when it was retired and flown to Le Bourget Airport to be displayed at the museum. Its final commercial service from Charles de Gaulle Airport was on 10 February 2000. It was opened to the public for display in June 2003, having accumulated 97,271 flight hours when it was retired. (Babak Taghvaee)

F-BVFB (c/n 207) was Air France's third Concorde, which operated from 8 April 1976 to 24 June 2003 when it flew to Karlsruhe, Germany, to be housed at the Technik Museum, Sinsheim. This photo of it was taken at Keflavik Naval Air Station on 27 September 1977. (US Department of Defense)

The seventh Aerospatiale Concorde supersonic passenger aircraft built for Air France. First flown on 26 December 1978 with r/c F-WJAN and c/n 215, this aircraft was finally delivered to Air France on 23 October 1980 with r/c F-BVFF and remained in service until 2003 when it was retired. Its four Rolls-Royce/Snecma Olympus 593 turbojet engines provided enough thrust for the aircraft to reach a 1,341mph (2,158km/h/1,165kn) cruise speed, almost twice that of any other Air France passenger aircraft in those years. With such speed, it could complete a transoceanic flight in almost four hours. The aircraft is currently preserved at Charles de Gaulle Airport. (Babak Taghvaee)

F-BVGA (c/n 5) became the first Airbus A300B2-1C delivered to Air France. Equipped with a pair of General Electric CF6-50C2 Turbofan engines, the wide-body airliner first flew on 15 April 1974 and was delivered on 10 May 1974. It is at Athens in 1976. (EX/ZX Collection)

Air France has operated 11 different Airbus A310 wide-body passenger aircraft, comprising seven 203 series and four 304 series. F-GEMF (c/n 172) was sold in 1994; the remaining ten were later retired and replaced with Airbus A330-203s in 2002 and 2003. This image shows A310-203 with r/c F-GEMA at Frankfurt in the early 1990s. (EX/ZX Collection)

Air France has operated six different Airbus A340-211 and 24 different Airbus A340-300 series aircraft (eight 311s and 16 313s). The 313 series were stretched and had more powerful engines, thus carried more passengers and cargo than the 200 series. Air France received the 311 series between 1993 and 1995. Some were leased from Sabena and returned to the airline in 1997, while the rest were retired years before the retirement of the 313s. This image shows an Air France A340-313s with r/c F-GLZS at Saint Maarten-Princess Juliana in late 1990s. (EX/ZX Collection)

Air France operated nine different Boeing 767-300ER series wide-body and long-haul passenger aircraft between 1991 and 2003. F-GHGJ is a Boeing 767-328ER operated between 28 May 1993 and 28 June 2002. Boeing 767s were replaced by Boeing 777-228ERs in the Air France fleet between 1998 and 2003. (EX/ZX Collection)

Air France Industries KLM Engineering & Maintenance is a major multi-product maintenance, repair and overhaul provider. It has a workforce of more than 12,800, supporting almost 3,000 aircraft operated by 200 major airlines. Its facility at Charles de Gaulle Airport is responsible for maintenance checks. These images show some of its maintenance hangars at Charles de Gaulle Airport. (Babak Taghvaee)

Chapter 1
The Narrow-Body Fleet

The Airbus A220-300 Fleet Since 2021

Airbus A220-300 single-aisle and narrow-body airliners are the backbone of Air France's fleet of jetliners and are used for short and medium-haul passenger services. On 30 July 2019, Air France signed a memorandum of understanding to buy 60 from Airbus. The aircraft was selected as a future replacement for the Airbus A318 and A319 narrow-body airliners for the airline's short and medium-haul network. An aircraft with significantly lower operational costs could allow Air France to compete with European low-cost airlines in the market from 2021, when deliveries of the aircraft began.

The A220 dates back to the early 1990s, when design and development began by Canadian Bombardier Inc. After Dutch aircraft manufacturer Fokker declared bankruptcy in 1996, this provided an opportunity for Bombardier to launch project BRJ-X (Bombardier Regional Jet Expansion) on 8 September 1998. The project aimed to design and develop a narrow-body aircraft capable of competing with or replacing narrow-body jetliners with a 2 x 3 seat-configured cabin such as the DC-9, MD-80, Boeing 717 and also with 3 x 3 seat configuration such as the Airbus A318, Boeing 737-500 and Boeing 737-600. Two years later, the BRFJ-X plan was shelved in favour of another aircraft, the CRJ-900, which was a stretched variant of the CRJ-700.

On 8 March 2004, Bombardier began studying plans to produce two CSeries jetliners, resulting in the creation of two variants, one named C100 with 110–115 seats, and the other named C130 with 130–135 seats, both in 2 x 3 seating arrangement in the cockpit. The CSeries jetliners were to be manufactured as a replacement for the DC-9/MD-80 and Boeing 737 Classic family, but also for Fokker 100 and BAe-146, as well as Avro RJ70/85/100s.

On 15 March 2005, marketing of the CSeries was authorised by the Bombardier's board of directors in order to seek firm commitments before the launch of the programme, which in May of that year was reported to have an estimated total development value of US$2.1bn. The cost was going to be shared equally by three suppliers and partner governments. The governments of Canada, Quebec, and the United Kingdom each invested US$87.5 million and US$340 million (£180 million) respectively.

Two years later, Bombardier finally selected the P&W geared turbofan (GTF engine, now the PW1500G) for the CSeries, rated at 23,000lbf (100kN) in November 2007. In March 2009, the C110 and C130 designation of the CSeries aircraft was changed to CS100 and CS300 respectively by Bombardier. The aircraft were offered in standard and extended range (ER) variants and there was also an extra thrust (XT) variant of the CS300 although ultimately Bombardier settled on a single variant, making the ER (extended range) a new standard.

Construction of the first CS100 prototype began in 2009. The aircraft was finished in 2013 and logged its maiden flight from Bombardier's facility at Montréal–Mirabel International Airport in Quebec on 16 September 2013. Flight testing lasted until 2015. As the certification tests were delayed, the entry-in-service date, which was planned for 16 January 2014, was delayed for more than a year. In 2013 and 2014, three more flight test vehicles (FTVs) or prototypes were built. These four CS100 FTVs accumulated more than 1,000 flight hours by 20 February 2015. On 27 February 2015, the first C300 prototype logged its maiden flight from Mirabel Airport. A fifth CS100 was also completed that year and logged its first flight on 18 March. By mid-2015, certification tests for the CS100s were finished. In June of that year, Bombardier released updated performance data about the CS100 and CS300, drawing the attention of Air France.

The first CSeries, a CS100, was delivered to Swiss Global Air Lines on 29 June 2016 at Montréal-Mirabel International Airport. The aircraft was put into commercial service on a flight between Zürich and Paris on 15 July. Almost six months before that, CS100 had received a type certificate from Transport Canada on 18 December 2015. Type certificates were also received from the US Federal Aviation Administration (FAA) and European Aviation Safety Agency (EASA) in June 2016. The larger CS300, capable of carrying 130 to 145 passengers, obtained type certificates from Transport Canada, EASA and FAA on 11 July, 7 October and 14 December 2016 respectively. The first CS300 was delivered to airBaltic on 28 November 2016 and was put into service with a 145-seat, two-class configuration between Riga and Amsterdam on 14 December 2016.

PW1500G engine delivery delays led to delayed production and delivery of the CS100s and CS300s. In 2016, just seven aircraft were delivered to both of the launch operators, Swiss Airlines and Air Baltic, followed by 17 more in 2017. On 1 July 2018, when the Airbus partnership came into effect, 37 aircraft had already been delivered. The CSeries competed with the A319neo (new engine option), a smaller member of the A320neo family. In February 2020, Bombardier exited the A220 programme a month after reassessing its participation. It sold its share to Airbus for US$591m, allowing Airbus to own 75 per cent of the programme. Under the terms of acquisition, Airbus also obtained Bombardier's option of buying out Investissement Québec's share from 2023, with a revised option date of 2026.

Financial issues at Bombardier over the CSeries programme and production delays, as well as competition with other aircraft, led to a partnership with Airbus on 1 July 2018. Ten days later, the CSeries CS100 and CS300 were rebranded as Airbus A220-100 and 300. On 20 July 2018, the first aircraft with Airbus branding, an A220-300, was delivered to the type launch operator airBaltic.

Upon their introduction in 2016, both the CS100 and CS300 performed above their original specifications. The CS100 and CS300 were determined to be one and three per cent more fuel-efficient than the figures announced by the manufacturer. In addition, the CS300 burned 20 per cent less fuel than the Airbus A319ceo and 21 per cent less than the Boeing 737 Classic, while the CS100 burned 18–27 per cent less per seat than the Avro RJ100. Furthermore, the CS300 is 6 tonnes (13,000lb) lighter than the Airbus A319neo and nearly eight tonnes (18,000lb) lighter than the Boeing 737 MAX 7, giving it an operating cost advantage of up to 12 per cent.

In July 2019, the Air France-KLM Group and Airbus signed a memorandum of understanding to order 60 A220-300s as future replacements for Air France's A318/A319 aircraft. In December 2019, the order was confirmed.

Deliveries to Air France

The A220-300s were intended to replace 18 of Air France's A318s and 33 A319s between 2021 and 2025. Deliveries started with F-HZUA (c/n 55134) on 20 September 2021. The aircraft, which first flew in Montreal on 26 August 2021, was later given the name *Le Bourget*. It was flown to Charles de Gaulle Airport, Paris, on 29 September 2021.

From 31 October 2021, F-HZUA flew to Berlin, Barcelona, Madrid, Milan-Linate and Venice from the Air France hub in Paris. During the 2021–22 winter season, Air France gradually extended its A220 flights to Bologna, Rome, Lisbon and Copenhagen as more aircraft were delivered.

Five more aircraft with r/c F-HZUB to F-HZUF were delivered on 5 November, 1 November, 15 December, 29 November and 17 December 2021. They were named *Saint-Jean-de-Luz*, *Senlis*, *Lesparre-Médoc*, *Giverny* and *Saint-Tropez*.

In 2022, 12 more A220-300s were delivered. They were F-HZUG (c/n 55155) *Provins*, F-HZUH (c/n 55157) *Rocamadour*, F-HZUI (c/n 55159) *Arcachon*, F-HZUJ (c/n 55171) *Auvers-sur-Oise*, F-HZUK (c/n 55173) *Belle-Île-en-Mer*, F-HZUL (c/n 55174) *Sarlat-la-Canéda*, F-HZUM (c/n 55185) named *Bayeux*, F-HZUN (c/n 55187) *Briançon*, F-HZUR (c/n 55198) *Collioure* and F-HZUS (c/n 55200) *Chinon*. They were delivered on 25 February, 18 March, 6 May, 22 June, 21 July, 15 July, 28 October, 8 November, 29 November and 31 December 2022.

In summer 2022, the Air France Airbus A220-300s served Berlin, Hamburg and Munich; Milan-Linate, Milan-Malpensa, Bologna, Rome, Naples and Venice; Barcelona, Valencia and Madrid; Lisbon; Copenhagen; Athens; Helsinki; Vienna; Warsaw; and Stockholm on departure from the Air France hub at Charles de Gaulle Airport.

Twelve more aircraft were delivered in the first two quarters of 2023. They were F-HZUO (c/n 55193) *Les Baux-de-Provence*, F-HZUP (c/n 55196) *Honfleur*, F-HZUQ (c/n 55197) *Bonifacio*, F-HZUT (c/n F-HZUT) *Bandol*, F-HZUU (c/n 55213) *Grasse*, F-HZUV (c/n 55216) *Châteauneuf-du-Pape*, F-HZUX (c/n 55218) *Meursault*, F-HZUY (c/n 55221) *Nuits-Saint-George*s, F-HZUZ (c/n 55223) *Paulliac*, F-HPNA (c/n 55227) *Saumur*, F-HPNB (c/n 55229) *Sauternes* and F-HPNC (c/n 55230) *Gaillac*. Their deliveries took place on 15 March, 5 April, 29 March, 28 April, 26 April, 26 May, 6 June, 1 August, 20 July and 6 July 2023.

Two more A220-300s with c/n 55232 and 55233, which first flew on 2 and 9 July 2023, were delivered to Air France in August 2023. Their deliveries led to an increase to 30 of the number of A220-300s in Air France service, leaving 30 more to be delivered by the end of 2025. By the end of 2023, Air France's remaining A318s were retired, while the A319s were expected to retire in 2024.

Crew Training and Operations

In September 2020, eight instructor pilots from Air France attended an eight-week theoretical and practical training course at the Airbus training centre in Montreal. With the delivery of the first A220-300 in July 2021, they began training colleagues – including another 28 instructors who completed the pilot launch team – notably using a Full Flight Simulator (FFS) mounted on jacks and assembled at Air France's flight simulation centre at Paris Charles de Gaulle.

Once Air France took delivery of the first A220, the simulator training was supplemented by approximately 20 flights in real conditions, with a view to obtaining the A220-300 type rating. It was intended that 700 Air France pilots would eventually be qualified to fly this aircraft, trained over four years.

Fourteen flight attendants were trained in Zurich between September and December 2020. The core group selected and trained a group of 37 flight attendants to complete the practical cabin-crew flight training as soon as the A220 entered service. Two A220 door models were installed at the Air France Crew Academy at Paray Vieille-Poste, near Paris-Orly, to train 2,500 flight attendants.

As it is made with lighter composite materials, the Airbus A220 uses 20 per cent less fuel than previous generation aircraft, and has a 34 per cent reduced noise footprint. It has so far played a decisive role in achieving Air France's sustainable development objectives, including a 50 per cent reduction in CO_2 emissions in absolute terms on the domestic network from Paris-Orly and on inter-regional routes by 2024, and a 50 per cent reduction in CO_2 emissions per passenger/km by 2030.

The Air France Airbus A220-300s have a cabin configuration with 148 seats, in a 3 x 2 seat configuration (five seats across the aircraft width) offering 80 per cent of customers a window or aisle seat. It offers two travel cabins, Business and Economy, and access to Air France Connect, the airline's inflight Wi-Fi service.

This image shows the second Air France A220-300 with r/c F-HZUB (c/n 55139) named *Saint-Jean-de-Luz* on the 26R runway of Charles de Gaulle Airport ready for take-off on 9 June 2022. (Babak Taghvaee)

F-HZUC (c/n 55140), the third A220-300 owned by Air France, is leaving Charles de Gaulle Airport for Rome with flight AF1304 on 23 June 2023. (Babak Taghvaee)

F-HZUD (c/n 55141), the fourth A220-300, is departing Paris for Helsinki (flight AF1176) on 23 June 2023. (Babak Taghvaee)

F-HZUE (c/n 55146), the fifth A220-300, is departing Paris Charles de Gaulle Airport (flight AF1800) for Madrid on 2 August 2023. (Babak Taghvaee)

F-HZUH (c/n 55157) is departing Paris Charles de Gaulle Airport for Copenhagen (flight AF1350) on 23 June 2023. (Babak Taghvaee)

F-HZUI (c/n 55159) is departing Paris Charles de Gaulle Airport for London (flight AF1780) on 2 August 2023. (Babak Taghvaee)

Above: F-HZUL (c/n 55174) is arriving at Paris Charles de Gaulle Airport with a flight from Berlin (AF1734) on 2 August 2023. (Babak Taghvaee)

Right: F-HZUM (c/n 55185) is leaving Paris Charles de Gaulle Airport for Milan (flight AF1732) on 23 June 2023. (Babak Taghvaee)

Below: F-HZUN (c/n 55187) has landed on runway 26L of Paris Charles de Gaulle Airport after a flight from Montpellier (AF7461) on 2 August 2023. (Babak Taghvaee)

F-HZUO (c/n 55193) named *Les Baux-de-Provence* is at Paris Charles de Gaulle Airport on 25 April 2023. It has been in service with Air France since February 2023. (Babak Taghvaee)

F-HZUR (c/n 55198) is departing Paris Charles de Gaulle Airport for Warsaw (flight AF1246) on 23 June 2023. (Babak Taghvaee)

Named *Bandol*, F-HZUT (c/n 55210) is arriving at Paris Charles de Gaulle Airport with a flight from Madrid (flight AF1300) on 2 August 2023. (Babak Taghvaee)

F-HZUV (c/n 55216) is at Paris Charles de Gaulle Airport, arriving from London (flight AF1781), on 23 June 2023. The aircraft, named *Chateauneuf-du-Pape*, was delivered to Air France on 28 April 2023. (Babak Taghvaee)

The A318 Fleet Between 2003 and 2023

The A220-300s are scheduled to take the place of the Airbus A318-111 passenger aircraft in Air France service. The A318 is the smallest and least numerous variant of the Airbus A320 family. It is more than 6m shorter and around 3 tonnes (6,600lbs) lighter than the A320. To compensate for the reduced moment arm*, it has a larger vertical stabiliser. Designed to carry between 107 and 132 passengers in 3 x 3 seat arrangements, the aircraft has a maximum range of 5,750km (3,100 nautical miles/3,570 miles). Air France operated them with 131 seats primarily for short-range service. Due to its similarity to the A320, the two aircraft shared a common type rating with all other A320 family variants, allowing A320 pilots to fly the aircraft without the need for further training.

A total of 81 A318s were built; among them 18 were delivered to Air France between 2003 and 2007, making the airline its largest operator. Deliveries started with F-GUGA (c/n 2035) on 9 October 2003 at Hamburg, where the aircraft were assembled and built. Air France's aircraft are powered by the CFM56-5B model. CFM56 engines are produced by CFM International (CFM). In that year, Air France received four more A318-111s, which were F-GUGB (c/n 2059), F-GUGC (c/n 2071), F-GUGD (c/n 2081) and F-GUGE (c/n 2100) that had been first flown on 15 October, 24 October, 7 November and 3 December respectively. They were delivered on 7 November, 21 November, 5 December and 17 December respectively.

In 2004, four more A318-111s were delivered. They were F-GUGF (c/n 2109), F-GUGG (c/n 2317), F-GUGH (c/n 2344) and F-GUGI (c/n 2350), which had been first flown on 13 January, 7 October, 4 November, and 10 November 2004 respectively. In order, they were delivered on 4 February, 29 October, 6 December, and 13 December of that year. In 2005, F-GUGJ (c/n 2582), and F-GUGK (c/n 2601), which were first flown on 5 and 25 October 2005, were delivered on 14 October and 9 November 2005.

In 2006, F-GUGL (c/n 2686), F-GUGM (c/n 2750), F-GUGN (c/n 2918), F-GUGO (c/n 2951) and F-GUGP (c/n 2967) were delivered on 22 February, 13 April, 26 October, 27 November and 14 December. They were first flown on 8 February, 3 April, 17 October, 15 November and 5 December 2006. The last two aircraft, F-GUGQ (c/n 2972) and F-GUGR (c/n 3009) were first flown in Hamburg on 8 December 2006 and 17 January 2007 and were delivered on 11 January and 22 February 2007 respectively.

With the delivery of the first A220-300 in 2021, retirement of the A318s began. The first aircraft was F-GUGA, which was retired on 29 October 2021, after its last flight from Nice to Orly. It was scrapped at Cotswold Airport later. In 2021, five more aircraft were retired. They were F-GUGB (on 12 September), F-GUGC (on 5 November), F-GUGD (on 14 October), F-GUGE (on 7 November) and F-GUGF (on 6 December). They were flown to storage facilities on 26 October 2021, 20 December 2021, 11 December 2021, 10 January 2022 and 6 January 2022.

In 2022, F-GUGG, F-GUGH and F-GUGI were retired on 14 October, 13 June and 20 October, respectively. They were flown to storage facilities on 14 October, 15 July and 13 December 2022, respectively. So far F-GUGI, which was stored at Saint Athan, UK, has been scrapped.

F-GUGJ, F-GUGK, F-GUGL and F-GUGR logged their last flights for Air France on 23 April, 10 July, 12 June and 28 July 2023. The F-GUGJ and F-GUGK were flown to the storage facilities after their retirement on 10 July and 1 August 2023, while the other two were kept in Toulouse (F-GUGL) and Charles de Gaulle Airport (F-GUGK) awaiting ferry flights to storage facilities as of August 2023. Between 4 and 8 August, F-GUGM, F-GUGP and F-GUGQ logged their last flights, while F-GUGO and F-GUGN remained in service for a few more days.

---

* The moment arm is the distance from a reference point or line to the applied force.

F-GUGE (c/n 2100) was an A318-111 operated by Air France between 17 December 2003 and 7 November 2021. It is at Charles de Gaulle Airport on 1 January 2021. (Babak Taghvaee)

This Air France A318-111, with r/c F-GUGH (c/n 2344), was operated by the airline between 6 December 2004 and 13 June 2022. It flew to Griffiss International Airport, USA, on 15 July 2022, and it was scrapped later. (Babak Taghvaee)

F-GUGI (c/n 2350) was another A318-111. Air France operated it between 6 December 2004 and 13 June 2022. It later flew to Griffiss International Airport, on 15 July 2022, and was later scrapped there. In this photo, it can be seen at Paris Charles de Gaulle on 21 September 2020. (Babak Taghvaee)

This A318-111 with r/c F-GUGJ (c/n 2582) was operated by Air France between 14 October 2005 and 23 April 2023. It flew to Twente, Netherlands, on 10 July 2023 and was scrapped there later. (Babak Taghvaee)

F-GUGN (c/n 2918) was one of the last A318-111s that Air France operated until the end of 2023. The aircraft is at Paris Charles de Gaulle, arriving from Florence (flight AF1667) on 23 August 2023. (Babak Taghvaee)

Delivered on 27 November 2006, this A318-111 remained in service with Air France until the end of 2023. It is at Paris Charles de Gaulle Airport on 21 September 2020. (Babak Taghvaee)

The A319 Fleet Since 1997

The second aircraft type that the A220-300s are replacing in Air France's service, is the Airbus A319, another member of A320 family of aircraft. It is almost 4m (12ft) shorter than the A320 and almost 2m (8ft) longer than the A318. The A319ceo (conventional engine option) had a higher range than the A318s and A320s with conventional engines. While the range of A318 and A320 were 5,700km (3,100 nmi/3,600 miles) and 6,100km (3,300nmi/3,800 miles, the A319ceo could fly for a maximum 6,940km (3,750 nmi/4,320 miles).

With 142 passenger seats in two classes, the A319s were operated for short- and medium-range flights just like the A318s. These aircraft were used for flights inside the mainland as well as to other European destinations. The airline has operated three different series of A319s, the 111, 113 and 115. The 111 series had CFM56-5B5/P turbofan engines (each with 22,00lbf (98kN) thrust), the 113s had weaker CFM56-5A4 engines (also with 22,000lbf (98kN) thrust), and the 115s had slightly more powerful CFM56-5B7/P engines, (each with 27,00lbf (120kN) thrust).

Before receiving the A319-111s, Air France began using nine A319-113s previously leased from International Lease Finance Corporation (ILFC) by Air Inter. They were F-GPMA (c/n 598), F-GPMB (c/n 600), F-GPMC (c/n 608), F-GPMD (c/n 618), F-GPME (c/n 625), F-GPMF (c/n 637), F-GPMG (c/n 644), F-GPMH (c/n 647) and F-GPMI (c/n 660). They had been delivered to Air Inter between 15 June 1996 and 10 March 1997, but after the merger of the airline into Air France, they were put into Air France's service in September 1997.

In 1999, Air France began receiving A319-111s. That year, F-GRHA (c/n 938), F-GRHB (c/n 985), F-GRHC (c/n 998), F-GRHD (c/n 1000), F-GRHE (c/n 1020), F-GRHF (c/n 1025), F-GRHG (c/n 1036) and F-GRHH (c/n 1151) were delivered on 15 February, 18 March, 12 April, 14 April, 21 May, 15 June, 24 June and 22 December.

Deliveries continued in 2000 with eight more A319-111 arrivals. They were F-GRHI (c/n 1169) on 4 February, F-GRHJ (c/n 1176) on 2 March, F-GRHK (c/n 1190) on 14 March, F-GRHL (c/n 1201) on 3 April, F-GRHM (c/n 1216) on 24 May, F-GRHN (c/n 1267) on 10 July, F-GRHO (c/n 1271) on 13 July and F-GRHP (c/n 1344) on 20 October.

In 2001, 12 more A319-111s were delivered. They were F-GRHQ (c/n 1404) on 11 January, F-GRHR (c/n 1415) on 14 May, F-GRHS (c/n 1444) on 22 March, F-GRHT (c/n 1449) on 8 March, F-GRHU (c/n 1471) on 5 April, F-GRHV (c/n 1505) on 30 May, F-GRHX (c/n 1524) on 26 June, F-GRHY (c/n 1616) on 15 November, F-GRHZ (c/n 1622) on 23 November, F-GRXA (c/n 1640) on 14 December and F-GRXB (c/n 1645) on 19 December.

Over the following years, more were delivered. F-GRXC (c/n 1677), F-GRXD (c/n 1699), F-GRXE (c/n 1733) were delivered on 19 February, 21 March and 8 May 2002, followed by F-GRXF (c/n 1938) on 25 March 2003. Later, F-GRXG (c/n 2213), F-GRXH (c/n 2228), F-GRXI (c/n 2279) and F-GRXJ (c/n 2456) were delivered on 10 June 2004, 10 June 2004, 13 September 2004 and 20 April 2005, respectively. Two more A319-111s with F-GRXM (c/n 2961) and F-GRXL (c/n 2938) r/cs were received on 7 December 2006, followed by two A319-115s with F-GRXK (c/n 2716) and F-GRXN (c/n 3065) on 31 March 2006 and 2 April 2007, respectively.

The total number of A319s in service with the airline reached 59. Among them, several had been dry leased from various aircraft-leasing companies such as IFLC, while some were owned by the airline. In addition to these, a third A319-115 was operated by the airline for a short period of time. The aircraft with r/c F-GYAS and c/n 1999 was leased from CIT Aerospace, an aircraft leasing and advisory services organisation, which is part of CIT Group in the United States. The aircraft was leased from 22 January 2004 to January 2007.

Many of these leased A319s had their contracts terminated and were returned to their lessors, even though the order for the 60 A220-300s was placed in 2019. Eight of the A319-113s, with older CFM56-5A4 engines and inherited from Air Inter, were withdrawn from use between 2007 and 2019. F-GPMA and F-GPMB were retired on 24 March 2018, F-GPMC on 28 March 2018, F-GPME on 26 September 2018, F-GPMF on 6 January 2019, F-GPMG on 7 March 2008, F-GPMH on 7 February 2007 and F-GPMI on 9 March 2007. The last of the A319-113s was F-GMPD, which logged its last passenger-carrying flight on 16 March 2020 and was withdrawn from use on 14 December 2020.

As of August 2023, 25 A319-111s and one A319-115 had been withdrawn from use by the airline. The A319-115 with r/c F-GRXN, which was withdrawn from use on 16 April 2012, was returned to its lessor, ILFC. Those A319-111s that were withdrawn from use before 2022 were mostly leased from companies such as ILFC. Those leased aircraft have mostly found new uses with other airlines. Many of those previously owned by Air France have been scrapped in Saint Athan and other airfields due to having logged more cycles and flying hours than the leased aircraft, which were returned to their lessors just a few years after the start of their operations with Air France.

The retired A319-111s are F-GRHA (retired on 21 December 2014), F-GRHC (retired on 12 February 2015), F-GRHD (retired on 1 May 2015), F-GRHE (6 February 2022), F-GRHG (22 July 2021), F-GRHH (28 April 2023), F-GRHI (17 November 2022), F-GRHJ (5 April 2022), F-GRHL (29 November 2022), F-GRHM (27 January 2022), F-GRHO (21 December 2022), F-GRHQ (18 July 2023), F-GRHR (14 May 2020), F-GRHU (31 March 2021), F-GRHX (26 September 2022), F-GRXA (24 October 2022), F-GRXC (18 May 2022), F-GRXD (13 April 2023), F-GRXE (11 May 2022), F-GRXG (2 April 2021), F-GRXH (28 February 2021), F-GRXI (September 2010), F-GRXJ (30 August 2022), F-GRXL (30 November 2022) and F-GRXM (14 December 2022).

In August 2023, Air France had 13 A319-111s and an A319-115LR in use. The series 115LR (long-range) aircraft was F-GRXK, which was 17 years old, while the A319-111s were F-GRHB, F-GRHF, F-GRHK, F-GRHN, F-GRHP, F-GRHR, F-GRHS, F-GRHT, F-GRHV, F-GRHY, F-GRHZ, F-GRXB and F-GRXF. They were scheduled to be retired and replaced with more A220-300s by 2025.

F-GRHF (c/n 1025) is an Air France A319-111, which has been operated by the airline since 15 June 1999. It is at Paris Charles de Gaulle on 22 August 2021. (Babak Taghvaee)

Air France operated this A319-111 with r/c F-GRHM (c/n 1216) from 24 May 2000 to 8 September 2021 under a long-term leasing contract with ILFC. The aircraft now belongs to AerCap Holdings NV, a leasing company, with r/c EI-HCY. It is at Paris Charles de Gaulle on 22 August 2021. (Babak Taghvaee)

Left: This A319-111 has been operated by Air France since 10 July 2000. This aircraft with r/c F-GRHN (c/n 1267) is departing Paris Charles de Gaulle in January 2021. (Babak Taghvaee)

Below: F-GRHP (c/n 1344) is an A319-111 operated by Air France and is at Paris-Orly Airport, arriving from Algiers (flight AF7541) on 22 July 2023. (Babak Taghvaee)

Above: F-GRHT (c/n 1449) is an Air France A319-111, operated since 8 March 2001. The aircraft is landing at Paris Charles de Gaulle on flight number AF1423 from Munich. (Babak Taghvaee)

Right: F-GRHZ (c/n 1622) has been operated by Air France since 23 November 2001. It is departing Paris Charles de Gaulle on 25 December 2020. (Babak Taghvaee)

Below: F-GRXB (c/n 1645) (nearest) has been in use by Air France since 19 December 2001. It is at Paris-Orly Airport on 28 March 2022. (Babak Taghvaee)

F-GRXK (c/n 2716) has been in use by Air France since 31 March 2006. It is taking off from Paris Charles de Gaulle with flight AF1096 to Santorini on 2 August 2023. (Babak Taghvaee)

The A320 Fleet Since 1988

The Airbus A320 is the second most popular aircraft in the market of narrow-body jetliners after the Boeing 737. Dating back to the 1970s, the Airbus A320 first entered service with Air France on 28 March 1988, with passenger flight operations starting on 8 April 1988. Air France has operated 111 A320s, many of them on dry lease from aircraft-leasing companies. Three variants of the aircraft were operated by the airline, the 111 series as a replacement for its Boeing 727-228s, the 211 series as a replacement for Boeing 737-200/300/500 series aircraft, and the 214 series as a replacement for the 111 and 211 series A320s. In addition, several 216, 231 and 232 series A320s were wet leased for a short period of time by the airline. Today, 38 A320s are still in service with Air France.

While the Airbus A300 wide-body passenger aircraft was in the final stages of its development, Airbus began working on a project to design and develop narrow-body airliners to compete with Boeing and Douglas (McDonnell Douglas) products, particularly the Boeing 737 and DC-9 at that time. In June 1977, a new Joint European Transport (JET) programme was set up, established by British Aerospace (BAe), Aerospatiale, Dornier and Fokker. This project was considered the forerunner of Airbus A320, encompassing the 130–188-seat aircraft market, powered by two CFM56s.

The programme was later transferred to Airbus, leading to the creation of the single-aisle (SA) studies in 1980, led by the former leader of the JET programme, Derek Brown. From the start, the development of three variants of the aircraft began, which later led to the creation of the A319, A320 and A321 today. In February 1981, the project was re-designated as A320, an aircraft that could carry 150 passengers using fuel from wing tanks only.

On 24 March 1984, the programme was launched with 96 firm orders including 25 for Air France as its launch customer. The airline had signed a letter of intent for procurement of 25 A320s with an option for 25 more during the 1981 Paris Air Show. In the presence of then-French Prime Minister Jacques Chirac and the Prince and Princess of Wales, the first A320 was rolled out of the assembly line at Toulouse on 14 February 1987 and made its maiden flight on 22 February in three hours and 23 minutes. The flight test programme took 1,200 hours across 530 flights. The European Joint Aviation Authorities (JAA) certification was awarded on 26 February 1988. The first A320 was delivered to Air France on 28 March and began commercial service on 8 April with a flight between Paris and Berlin via Düsseldorf.

The first 14 A320s of Air France and Air Inter were 111 series and equipped with CFM56-5A1 turbofan engines. They were F-GFKQ (c/n 2), F-GGEG (c/n 3), F-GGEF (c/n 4), F-GFKA (c/n 5), F-GFKB (c/n 7), F-GFKC (c/n 9), F-GGEA (c/n 10), F-GGEB (c/n 12), F-GGEC (c/n 13), F-GFKD (c/n 14), F-GGEE (c/n 16), F-GFKE (c/n 19), F-GFKF (c/n 20) and F-GFKG (c/n 21). Their deliveries started with F-GFKA on 28 March 1988 and finished with F-GFKQ on 8 February 1991.

Among these aircraft, F-GGEA, F-GGEC, F-GGEE, F-GGEF, F-GGEG and F-GGEV were delivered to Air Inter but were incorporated into Air France service following the merger of the airlines in 1997. Air France retired its A320-111s from service between 2007 and 2009, having them replaced with A320-214s.

The newly delivered F-GFKC (c/n 9) was lost in a crash on 26 June 1988, killing its three crew and three passengers onboard during an air show at Mulhouse-Habsheim Airport, France. While performing a low pass below 100 feet altitude, the aircraft crashed into a forest and a fire broke out, killing all onboard.

The Winglet-Equipped A320-211s

Between 1989 and 1992, the airline received 23 more aircraft, all A320-211s. Key improvements of A320-211s over the 111 series were wingtip fences and increased fuel capacity, which provided increased range. The A320-211s had a pair of CFM56-5A1 engines similar to the A320-111s. In 1989, six of them were delivered; F-GHQA (c/n 33), F-GHQB (c/n 36), F-GHQC (c/n 44), F-GFKH (c/n 61), F-GFKI (c/n 62) and F-GFKJ (c/n 63) on 15 February, 16 March, 6 April, 1 June, 18 August and 1 September.

In 1990, six more A320-211s were delivered. They were F-GFKK (c/n 100), F-GFKL (c/n 101), F-GFKM (c/n 102), F-GHQD (c/n 108), F-GFKO (c/n 129) and F-GFKP (c/n 133) on 16 March, 2 February, 23 March, 31 May, 28 November and 10 December.

In 1991, eight more A320-211s were delivered. They were F-GFKN (c/n 128) on 8 January, F-GJVB (c/n 145) on 31 January, F-GFKR (c/n 186) on 3 May, F-GFKS (c/n 187) on 22 May, F-GFKT (c/n 188) on 29 May, F-GFKU (c/n 226) on 5 September, F-GFKV (c/n 227) on 10 September and F-GFKX (c/n 228) on 23 September. The following year, Air France received three more A320-211s, which were F-GFKY (c/n 285) on 28 February 1992, F-GFKZ (c/n 286) on 5 March 1992 and F-GKXA (c/n 287) on 13 March 1992.

In 1997, Air France inherited 21 A320-211s from Air Inter after its merger with the airline; 19 were owned by the airline while two had been leased. These 21 were F-GHQE (c/n 115), F-GHQF (c/n 130), F-GJVA (c/n 144), F-GHQG (c/n 155), F-GHQH (c/n 156), F-GHQI (c/n 184), F-GJVC (c/n 204), F-GJVD (c/n 211), F-GHQJ (c/n 214, F-GJVE (c/n 215), F-GHQK (c/n 236), F-GHQM (c/n 237), F-GHQL (c/n 239), F-GJVF (c/n 244), F-GJVG (c/n 270), F-GHQO (c/n 278), F-GHQP (c/n 337), F-GHQQ (c/n 352), F-GHQR (c/n 377), F-GJVU (c/n 436) and F-GJVW (c/n 491).

In addition to the 44 A320-211s, including the 21 inherited from Air Inter, Air France operated five other leased A320-211s for a short period of time. They were F-GLFM (c/n 131) between 2001–09, F-GLGG (c/n 203) between 1998–2008, F-GLGI (c/n 221) between 1994–98, F-GKXB (c/n 235) between 2001–11 and F-GJVU (c/n 436) between 1997–2004.

The CFM56-5B4/P-Engined A320-214s

In 2001, Air France started receiving A320-214s with improved CFM56-5B4/P turbofan engines. CFM56-5B series engines were originally designed for use on the A321 and a stretched variant of the A321 but were later widely used on the A320s. With a thrust range between 22,000 and 33,000lbf (98kN and 147kN), it can power every model in the A320 family (A318/A319/A320/A321) and has superseded the CFM56-5A series. Among the changes from the CFM56-5A is the option of a double annular combuster that reduces emissions (particularly NOx), a new fan in a longer fan case, and a new low-pressure compressor with a fourth stage (up from three in earlier variants). CFM56-5B4 has a 27,000lbf (120kN) thrust while CFM56-5A1 produced 25,000lbf (111kN) thrust.

F-GKXC (c/n 1502) became the first A320-214 to enter service with Air France on 10 July 2001. *Le Mans* had logged its first flight on 18 May 2001. In the following year, three more were delivered. They were F-GKXD (c/n 1873) on 11 July 2002, F-GKXE (c/n 1879) on 27 September 2002 and F-GKXF (c/n 1885) on 2 December 2002.

In 2003, Air France received five more A320-214s; F-GKXG (c/n 1894) on 21 January, F-GFKH (c/n 1924) on 13 February, F-GKXI (c/n 1949) on 19 March, F-GKXJ (c/n 1900) on 14 February and F-GKXK (c/n 2140) on 9 December 2003.

Between 2004 and 2009, 14 more were delivered. These were F-GKXL (c/n 2705) on 17 March 2006, F-GKXM (c/n 2721) on 30 March 2006, F-GKXN (c/n 3008) on 26 January 2007, F-GKXO (c/n 3420) on 7 March 2008, F-GKXP (c/n 3470) on 11 April 2008, F-GKXQ (c/n 3777) on 30 January 2009, F-GKXR (c/n 3795) on 24 February 2009, F-GKXS (c/n 3825) on 18 March 2009, F-GKXT (c/n 3859) on 29 November 2017, F-GKXU (c/n 4063) on 28 October 2009, F-GKXV (c/n 4084) on 14 December 2017, F-GKXY (c/n 4105) on 25 November 2009, F-GKXZ (c/n 4137) on 16 December 2009 and F-HEPA (c/n 4139) on 21 December 2009.

In 2010, Air France received six more, including F-HBNA (c/n 4335) on 1 July, F-HBNB (c/n 4402) on 8 September, F-HEPB (c/n 4241) on 26 March, F-HEPC (c/n 4267) on 28 April, F-HEPD (c/n 4295) on 17 May, and F-HEPE (c/n 4298) on 18 May.

In 2011, seven more were delivered. These were F-HBNC (c/n 4601) and F-HBND (c/n 4604) on 9 March, F-HBNE (c/n 4664) on 15 April, F-HBNF (c/n 4714) on 26 May, F-HBNG (c/n 4747) on 29 June, F-HBNH (c/n 4800) on 25 August, and F-HBNJ (c/n 4908) on 23 November.

Between 2012 and 2018, eight more were delivered: F-HBNK (c/n 5084) on 16 April 2012, F-HBNL (c/n 5129) on 21 May 2012, F-HEPF (c/n 5719) on 23 August 2013, F-HEPG (c/n 5802) on 18 October 2013, F-HEPH (c/n 5869) on 3 December 2013, F-HEPI (c/n 7713) on 7 July 2017, F-HEPJ (c/n 7873) on 20 October 2017, F-HEPK (c/n 8127) on 7 March 2018. In addition, the airline leased one more A320-214s – F-HZFM (c/n 5887), operational since 24 November 2020.

As of August 2023, 38 A320-214s were being operated by the airline. They had two cabin configurations, one for 174 passengers (36 business class seats and 138 economy class seats) and another for 178 passengers (18 business class seats and 160 economy class seats). They are F-GKXC, F-GKXG, F-GKXH, F-GKXI, F-GKXJ, F-GKXL, F-GKXM, F-GKXN, F-GKXO, F-GKXP, F-GKXQ, F-GKXR, F-GKXS, F-GKXT, F-GKXU, F-GKXV, F-GKXY, F-GKXZ, F-HBNB, F-HBND, F-HBNE, F-HBNF, F-HBNG, F-HBNH, F-HBNJ, F-HBNL, F-HEPA, F-HEPB, F-HEPC, F-HEPD, F-HEPE, F-HEPF, F-HEPG, F-HEPH, F-HEPI, F-HEPJ and F-HEPK. Many of those A320-214s no longer in use had their leasing contracts terminated.

The six aircraft with r/cs F-HEPF to F-HEPK are equipped with Sharklets, which is defined in the aircraft name – A320-214sl. These Sharklets help reduce fuel consumption.

F-GKXC (c/n 1502) is an A320-214 that has been in use with Air France since 10 July 2001 on a long-term leasing contract. It is taking off from Paris Charles de Gaulle Airport bound for Tunis on 9 August 2023. (Babak Taghvaee)

Air France operated this A320-214 with F-GKXK (c/n 2140) between 9 December 2003 and 29 August 2021. It is at Paris Charles de Gaulle Airport on 1 January 2021. (Babak Taghvaee)

This A320-214 with r/c F-GKXP (c/n 3470) belongs to SMBC Aviation Capital and has been leased by Air France on a long-term contract since 11 April 2008. It is at Moscow-Sheremetyevo Airport on 25 August 2017. (Babak Taghvaee)

Left: This Airbus A320-214 with r/c F-GKXT (c/n 3859) has been owned by IFLC and then AerCap Holdings NV, two aircraft leasing companies since 2009. It has been leased to Air France under a long-term contract since 6 May 2009. It is landing on 14 December 2021. (Babak Taghvaee)

Below: This A320-214 with r/c F-GKXU (c/n 4063) is at Paris Charles de Gaulle after a flight from Berlin (flight AF1835) on 23 June 2023. (Babak Taghvaee)

The Narrow-Body Fleet

Above: F-GKXZ (c/n 4137) is departing Paris Charles de Gaulle for Copenhagen (flight AF4148) on 2 August 2023. (Babak Taghvaee)

Right: F-HBNB (c/n 4402) is departing Paris Charles de Gaulle for Milan during flight AF1312 on 23 June 2023. (Babak Taghvaee)

Below: F-HBNG (c/n 4747) is an A320-214 owned by Air France, and in use by the airline since 29 June 2011. It is at Paris Charles de Gaulle on 14 December 2021. (Babak Taghvaee)

This A320-214 with r/c F-HBNJ (c/n 4747) has been in use by Air France since 23 November 2011. It is arriving at Paris-Orly Airport from Bastia (flight AF7593) on 22 July 2023. (Babak Taghvaee)

F-HBNL (c/n 5129) has been in use by Air France since 21 May 2012. It is landing at Paris Charles de Gaulle Airport on 21 September 2020. (Babak Taghvaee)

This A320-214 with r/c F-HEPC (c/n 4267) belongs to AerCap Holdings NV and has been leased to Air France under a long-term contract since 28 April 2010. Initially named *Aurillac*, and then *Basse-Terre*, the aircraft is arriving at Paris Charles de Gaulle after a flight from Zurich (flight AF1115) on 2 August 2023. (Babak Taghvaee)

F-HEPD (c/n 4295), an A320-214 has been in use by Air France since 17 May 2010. The aircraft belongs to AerCap Holdings NV. It is at Paris Charles de Gaulle Airport on 21 September 2021. (Babak Taghvaee)

A Sharklet-equipped A320-214 sl named *Cognac*. The aircraft has been in use by Air France since 23 August 2013. Sharklets help reduce fuel consumption. (Babak Taghvaee)

F-HEPI (c/n 7713) is another A320-214 sl painted in SkyTeam special colours. Aeroméxico, Air France, Delta Air Lines and Korean Air founded SkyTeam, an Airline Alliance, in June 2000. Since then, the membership has increased to 20. Members have some of their aircraft painted in SkyTeam colours and Air France has five aircraft painted this way. F-HEPI is departing Paris Charles de Gaulle for Tbilisi with flight AF1052, on 9 August 2023. (Babak Taghvaee)

F-HEPK (c/n 8127) is a Sharklet-equipped A320-214. It is seen at Paris Charles de Gaulle, having arrived from Mykonos (flight AF1073) on 9 August 2023. (Babak Taghvaee)

This A320-214 with r/c F-HZFM (c/n 5887) has been in use by Air France since 24 November 2020. The aircraft, named *Figari*, is at Paris Charles de Gaulle on 9 June 2022. (Babak Taghvaee)

The A321 Fleet Since 1997

Airbus's A321 is the stretched version of the A320 and is the largest of the A320 family. It was the first derivative of the A320. The final phase of its development began on 24 November 1988 when the A320 was at the beginning of its career with Air France. Production of the A321 began after commitments for 183 aircraft from ten customers were secured. The maiden flight of the Airbus A321 was on 11 March 1993, when the prototype, registration F-WWIA, flew with International Aero Engines (IAE) V2500 engines; the second prototype, equipped with CFM56-5B turbofans, flew in May 1993.

The fuselage was lengthened by a 4.27m (14ft) plug ahead of the wing and a 2.67m (8ft 9in) plug behind it, making the A321 6.94m (22ft 9in) longer than the A320. In addition to the stretched fuselage, the aircraft had double-slotted flaps and minor trailing edge modifications, which increased the wing area from 124m^2 (1,330sq ft) to 128m^2 (1,380sq ft). As the aircraft was relatively heavier than the A320, its centre fuselage and landing gears were reinforced to accommodate a 9,600kg (21,200lb) increase in maximum take-off weight, taking it to 83,000kg (183,000lb).

While Air France was the launch customer for the A320 in 1988, Lufthansa became the launch customer for the A321 in 1994. In the same year, Air Inter, one of three subsidiary companies of the Air France Group, began receiving A321-111s. In total, five were delivered to the airline; F-GMZA (c/n 498), F-GMZB (c/n 509), F-GMZC (c/n 521), F-GMZD (c/n 529) and F-GMZE (c/n 544), with deliveries taking place on 30 June 1994, 26 August 1994, 22 March 1995, 15 May 1995 and 16 October 1995. After Air Inter merged with Air France, all five A321-111s entered service with Air France with no change in their registration codes.

The A321-111 was the original derivative of the A321 with a shorter range compared to the 211 as it had no extra fuel tank in order to compensate for the increased weight over increased length. It had a maximum take-off weight of 83,000kg (183,000lb), thanks to a pair of CFM56-5B1 each with 30,000lbf (130kN) thrust. Only 90 A321s were manufactured as the production line was switched to the series 200 A321s in 1996. These newer aircraft were equipped with more powerful CFM56-5B3 powerplants, each with 33,000lbf (150kN) thrust and could carry more fuel, as the maximum take-off weight was increased to 93,000kg (205,000lb). Its development began in 1995 and its first example flew in December 1996 and entered service with Monarch Airlines in April 1997.

Air France was one of the first customers to receive the A321-200 series, which began on 16 May 1997. In total, the airline received 13 aircraft over six years. These, with their delivery dates, were F-GTAA (c/n 674), 16 May 1997; F-GTAB (c/n 675), 30 May 1997; F-GTAC (c/n 684), 20 June 1997; F-GTAD (c/n 777), 9 February 1998; F-GTAE (c/n 796), 17 March 1998; F-GTAF (c/n 761), 11 February 1998; F-GTAG (c/n 956), 12 February 1999; F-GTAH (c/n 1133), 7 December 1999; F-GTAI (c/n 1299), 17 August 2000; F-GTAJ (c/n 1476), 11 April 2001; F-GTAK (c/n 1658), 18 January 2002; F-GTAL (c/n 1691), 4 March 2002; and F-GTAM (c/n 1859), delivered on 4 June 2003.

Among them, 11 were A321-211s, while F-GTAE and F-GTAH were A321-212s. Between 1998 and 2007, Air France returned some of its A321-111s and A321-211s to their lessors including F-GTAA, F-GTAB and F-GTAC to GATX Leasing in 2002. Two years later, F-GTAF was returned to GATX Leasing and F-GTAG was returned to GECAS in the same year.

As a replacement for these A321-211s, ten brand new A321s were delivered between 2007 and 2011. These were F-GTAN (c/n 3051), 8 March 2007; F-GTAO (c/n 3098), 25 April 2007; F-GTAR (c/n 3401), 16 February 2008; F-GTAS (c/n 3419), 3 March 2008; F-GTAT (c/n 3441, 25 March 2008; F-GTAU (c/n 3814), 27 February 2008; F-GTAV (c/n 3884), 1 May 2009; F-GTAX (c/n 3930), 8 June 2009; F-GTAY (c/n 4251), 30 March 2010; and F-GTAZ (c/n 4901), delivered on 23 November 2011. Among these three were A321-211s and seven were A321-212s (F-GTAL, F-GTAN, F-GTAR, F-GTAV, F-GTAX, F-GTAY and F-GTAZ).

As of August 2023, Air France had 16 A321s still in use. Four were Airbus A321-111s (F-GMZA, F-GMZC *Nancy*, F-GMZD *Toulon* and F-GMZE *Rouen*. The A321-211s were: F-GTAD *Annecy*, F-GTAJ *Ajaccio*, F-GTAK *Meaux*, F-GTAM *Calvi*, F-GTAP *Rennes*, F-GTAQ *Clermont-Ferrand*, F-GTAS *Castres*, F-GTAT *Aurillac* and F-GTAU *Beaune*. The rest were A321-212s: F-GTAE, F-GTAY and F-GTAZ. Air France's A321s have 212 passenger seats, made up of 36 for business class and 176 for economy class.

F-GMZA (c/n 498), an Airbus A321-111 leased from FT Global Lease, has been in use by Air France since September 1997 when Air Inter was merged with the company. This 29-year-old aircraft is at Paris Charles de Gaulle, arriving from Marseille (flight AF7339) on 9 August 2023. (Babak Taghvaee)

F-GMZE (c/n 0544) was one of four Air France A321-111s in service in August 2023. It is departing Paris Charles de Gaulle and heading to Nice (flight AF7308) on 9 August 2023. (Babak Taghvaee)

Airbus A321-212 with r/c F-GTAD (c/n 0777) *Annecy* has been in use by Air France since 9 February 1998. It is at Paris Charles de Gaulle Airport, arriving from Lyon (flight AF7367) on 9 August 2023. (Babak Taghvaee)

Left: F-GTAE (c/n 0796), an A321-212, is the only Air France example carrying the SkyTeam livery. SkyTeam was formed in 2000 and Air France has been a member of this airline alliance since that date. This image shows F-GTAE landing in Paris with flight AF7305 from Nice on 9 August 2023. (Babak Taghvaee)

Below: This Airbus A321-211 with r/c F-GTAJ (c/n 1476) has been operated by Air France since 11 April 2001. It was leased to JOON between 23 March 2018 and July 2019. It is at Paris Charles de Gaulle on 9 June 2022. (Babak Taghvaee)

F-GTAM (c/n 1859) is an A321-211 named *Calvi*. It was delivered on 4 June 2003 and operated by JOON, a low-cost subsidiary of Air France between 23 March 2018 and 27 June 2019. It is at Paris Charles de Gaulle on 14 December 2021. (Babak Taghvaee)

Right: F-GTAP (c/n 3372) was delivered to Air France on 21 January 2008. This aircraft belongs to AerCap Holdings NV and has been leased under a long-term contract. It is landing in Paris with flight AF7501 from Nantes on 9 August 2023. (Babak Taghvaee)

Below: Fifteen-year-old F-GTAS (c/n 3419) has been operated by Air France since 3 March 2018. It was operated by JOON, a low-cost subsidiary of Air France, between 19 March 2018 and July 2019. It is departing Paris Charles de Gaulle with flight AF7369 to Lyon on 9 August 2023. (Babak Taghvaee)

Chapter 2
The Wide-Body Fleet

The Boeing 777-228ER fleet since 1998

Air France is currently the third largest operator of Boeing 777 twin-engined long-range wide-body passenger aircraft, which connect France to its overseas territories and to capital cities around the world. The first variant of the aircraft to enter service was the 200ER (Extended Range) series aircraft. It was an increased gross-weight variant of the Boeing 777-200 series aircraft with greater range and payload capability initially named 777-200IGW but later renamed 200ER.

The aircraft's prototype first flew on 7 October 1996 and received FAA and JAA certification on 17 January 1997. The launch customer for the aircraft was British Airways, which began operating it from 9 February 1997. With its significantly improved and greater long-haul performance, the Boeing 777-200ER series aircraft became the most popular variant of the twin-engined airliner and was widely ordered in the early 2000s.

The value of a new -200ER rose from US$110m at service entry to US$130m in 2007; a 2007 model 777 sold for US$30 million ten years later. Air France placed an order for 25 Boeing 777-200ERs with deliveries between 1998 and 2001, which replaced the Airbus A340-211, 212, 311 and 312 long-range and wide-body passenger aircraft that had entered service between 1993 and 1995. This decision was made due to fuel consumption.

Air France's B777-200ERs were designated as model 228ER. They were equipped with General Electric GE90-94B high-bypass turbofan engines, each with 81,070–97,300lbf (360.6–432.8kN) take-off thrust. With Air France, they received F-GSPA to F-GSPZ registration codes.

With a length of 63.73m (209ft 1in) and 60.93m (199 ft 11in) wingspan, the aircraft had two types of cabin configurations. Some had 200 passenger seats (48 business seats, 32 premium economy seats and 120 economy seats), while others had 312 seats (28 business seats, 24 premium economy seats and 260 economy seats).

The first B777-228ER was delivered to Air France on 27 March 1998, two weeks after its first flight at the Boeing Company's factory in Seattle (on 12 March 1998). The aircraft with c/n 29002/129 received r/c F-GSPA. The airline received two more aircraft on 21 April 1998 and 5 May 1998, which were F-GSPB (c/n 29003/133) and F-GSPC (c/n 29004/138) and had first flown on 6 and 27 April 1998.

In 1999, Air France received seven more B777-228ERs, which were F-GSPD (c/n 29005/187), F-GSPE (c/n 29006/189), F-GSPF (c/n 29007/201), F-GSPG (c/n 27609/195), F-GSPH (c/n 28675/210), F-GSPI (c/n 29008/258) and F-GSPJ (c/n 29009/263). They were delivered on 12 January, 19 January, 11 March, 12 February, 21 May, 6 and 22 December 1999 respectively.

In 2000, four more B777-228ERs, with F-GSPK (c/n 29010/267), F-GSPL (c/n 30457/284), F-GSPM (c/n 30456/307) and F-GSPN (c/n 29011/314) r/cs were delivered on 27 January, 9 December, 14 November and 15 May. They were followed by five more in 2001, which were F-GSPO (c/n 30614/320) on 3 February, F-GSPP (c/n 30615/327) on 28 February, F-GSPQ (c/n 28682/331) on 21 March, F-GSPR (c/n 28683/367) on 19 October and F-GSPS (c/n 32306/370) on 2 November.

In 2002, Air France received six more B777-228ERs, which were F-GSPT (c/n 32308/382) on 22 January, F-GSPU (c/n 32309/383) on 1 February, F-GSPV (c/n 28684/385) on 15 February 2002, F-GSPX (c/n 32698/392) on 13 March, F-GSPY (c/n 32305/395) on 2 April and F-GSPZ (c/n 32310/401) on 17 July.

The relatively smaller fleet of B777-228ERs were more active during the Covid-19 pandemic. They were used on routes previously flown by the B777-328ERs. Air France began retiring some of its leased Boeing 777s with high flying hours and cycles, returning them to their lessors. Lessors included AerCap Holdings NV, ILFC and BBAM (Babcock and Brown Aircraft Management). Seven B777-228ERs, including F-GSPH, F-GSPR, F-GSPV, F-GSPB, F-GSPC, F-GSPS and F-GSPT, were retired on 29 March 2021, 25 April 2021, 11 February 2021, 14 July 2022, 15 March 2022, 15 March 2022, 16 March 2021 and 14 April 2022 respectively.

Four of the B777-228ERs that had the highest flying hours and cycles were sold to Tarmac Aerosave, including three with r/c F-GSPR, F-GSPV and F-GSPS, which had already been scrapped at Tarbes/Lourdes, France, and Teruel Airport in Spain. F-GSPC, which has logged 106,600 flying hours and 13,987 cycles, each with an average flight time of 7.62 hours, is currently waiting to be scrapped.

Among the 18 aircraft, only r/c F-GSPL is currently leased by Air France, while the rest are owned by it. Eight of the 18 B777-228ERs currently in service with the airline are named after French towns. They are F-GSPF *Compiègne*, F-GSPL *Biarritz*, F-GSPO *Saint-Germain-En-Laye*, F-GSPP *Montpellier*, F-GSPY *Vincennes*, F-GSPU *Saint-Etienne*, F-GSPZ *Villandry* and F-GSPX *Etretat*.

Above: **B777-228ER with r/c F-GSPE (c/n 29006) is taxiing at Paris-Charles de Gaulle after a flight from Boston (flight AF321) on 23 June 2023. (Babak Taghvaee)**

Right: **F-GSPG (c/n 27609), a B777-228ERs is departing Paris Charles de Gaulle for Dubai (flight AF662) on 23 June 2023. (Babak Taghvaee)**

F-GSPJ (c/n 29009) is a B777-228ER, which was delivered on 22 December 1999. It is at Paris Charles de Gaulle on 21 September 2020. (Babak Taghvaee)

This B777-228ER with r/c F-GSPL (c/n 30457) is departing Paris Charles de Gaulle for San Francisco (flight AF82) on 9 August 2023. (Babak Taghvaee)

F-GSPQ (c/n 28682) is a B777-228ER in use with Air France since 21 March 2001. It is at Paris Charles de Gaulle Airport on 18 April 2021, when it was still temporarily stored due to restrictions imposed on air travel during the Covid-19 pandemic. (Babak Taghvaee)

F-GSPS (c/n 32306) is a B777-228ERs, which was retired during the Covid-19 pandemic. The aircraft, which was delivered on 2 November 2001, performed its last commercial flight on 4 February 2021 before being sent to a storage facility on 16 March 2021. It was scrapped by Tarmac Aerosave in August 2021. The aircraft was owned by ILFC and had been leased under a long-term leasing contract. It is seen here at Paris Charles de Gaulle Airport while being towed on 5 February 2021. (Babak Taghvaee)

F-GSPX (c/n 32698), a Boeing 777-228ER operated by Air France since 13 March 2002. It is departing Paris Charles de Gaulle Airport on 25 December 2020. (Babak Taghvaee)

F-GSPZ (c/n 32310) is a B777-228ER. It was first flown in the US on 24 April 2002 and was delivered to Air France on 17 July 2002. It is departing Paris Charles de Gaulle Airport for Montreal (flight AF349) on 23 June 2023. (Babak Taghvaee)

The Airbus A330-203 Fleet Since 2001

Air France has operated Airbus A330-203 twin-engine wide-body and long-haul passenger aircraft since 2001. A total of 16 A330-203s, each equipped with a pair of General Electric CF6-80E1A3 turbofan engines, were purchased as a replacement for the ageing fleet of Airbus A300 and A310 wide-body passenger aircraft. The aircraft with r/c F-GZCA to F-GZCO were delivered to the airline between 20 December 2001 and 4 April 2005. Among these, one aircraft with r/c F-GZCP crashed en-route to Galeão International Airport, Rio de Janeiro from Charles de Gaulle Airport in the Atlantic Ocean, north-east of Fernando de Noronha islands, Brazil, killing all of its 228 occupants on 1 June 2009.

The A330 dates back to the mid-1970s when Airbus began development of the A300B9, a larger derivative of the A300. It was a lengthened A300 with the same wing, coupled with the most powerful turbofan engine available at that time. It was being developed to meet the growing need for wide-body passenger aircraft to serve high-capacity, medium-range, transcontinental routes. It was intended to compete with tri-engined McDonnell Douglas DC-10 and Lockheed L-1011 TriStar aircraft, which had 25 per cent better fuel consumption compared with twin engined aircraft.

While the A300B9 was intended to be a future medium-range replacement for the medium-range A300B2s, a B11 variant was also developed to be a replacement for long-range A300B4s. It was designed to have four engines and later became the Airbus A340, an aircraft that was intended to also replace narrow-body, long-haul Boeing 707s and Douglas DC-8s. Later the B9 and B11 names for these two aircraft were changed to TA9 and TA11 (TA prefix stood for twin aisle); both were capable of carrying a maximum 410 passengers. With necessary funding available, the Airbus Supervisory Board approved the development of the TA9 as the A330 and the TA11 as the A340 with potential customers on 27 January 1986. In that year, Airbus hoped five airlines would sign contracts for both the A330 and A340, and sent out sale proposals to the most likely candidates, including Lufthansa and Swissair.

On 12 March 1987, Airbus received its first orders for the twinjet. Domestic French airline Air Inter placed five firm orders and 15 options, while Thai Airways International requested eight aircraft, split evenly between firm orders and options. Design and development of the A330 alongside the A340 continued for four more years until production of the first prototypes began. The first A330 was completed and rolled out on 14 October 1992, with the first flight was on 2 November.

With a weight of 181,840kg (401,000lb), including 20,980kg (46,300lb) of test equipment, it became the largest twin-engined passenger aircraft jet at that time. On 21 October 1993, the Airbus A330 received European Joint Aviation Authorities (JAA) and the US Federal Aviation Administration (FAA) certifications after logging 1,114 hours of test flights in 426 cycles.

An A330 used for certification tests of the Pratt & Whitney turbofan engines crashed on 30 June 1994, killing both test pilots and five Airbus employees. An investigation by the French Aviation Authority (Direction Générale d'Aviation) determined that the cause of the accident was the slow response and incorrect action of the crew during recovery while testing the autopilot response during a one-engine-off worst-case scenario, with the centre of gravity near its aft limit. As a result of that accident, the A330's operating procedures were revised.

A Replacement for the A300s and A310s

On 17 January 1994, Air Inter, a subsidiary of the Air France Group, became the first airline to put an A330 into service. Two years later, Air France began retiring its A300 wide-body passenger aircraft and selected the A330 as its replacement. An order was placed for 16 A330-203s equipped with General Electric CF6-80E1A3 turbofan engines, an improved variant of those in use with the A300/310s. The A330-200 series aircraft was a shorter variant of the A330-300, which first flew in 1998. The A330-300 has a range of

11,750km (6,350nmi/7,300 miles) with 277 passengers, while the shorter A330-200 can cover 13,450km (7,250nmi/8,360 miles) with 247 passengers.

While the first A330 was delivered to Air France in 2001, the A300s were all retired before that. They were three A300B2-1Cs with r/c F-BVGA, F-BVGB and F-BVGC, an A300B4-2C with F-GLOC, and seven A300B4-203s with r/c F-BVGG, F-BVGH, F-BVGJ, F-BVGL, F-BVGN, F-BVGO and F-BVGT. F-BVGA, F-BVGB and F-BVGC with c/n 5, 6 and 7 had been operated by the airline since 10 May, 28 June and 10 August 1974 as replacements for the airline's Boeing 707s. These three were retired in 1997, 1998 and 1999 respectively.

The A300B2-100 series aircraft had been designed with Air France's requirement for more seats. With its more powerful engine compared to the A300B1, the aircraft was 2.6m (8½ft) longer than the A300B1 and had an increased maximum take-off weight of 137 tonnes (302,000lb), allowing for 30 additional seats and bringing the typical passenger count up to 281, with capacity for 20 LD3 containers. Following production of two prototypes, which made their first flight on 28 June 1973, the aircraft type received its certification on 15 March 1974.

F-GZCA (c/n 422) and F-GZCB (c/n 443) were the first two aircraft to be delivered on 20 December and 17 December 2001 respectively. Eight more were delivered in 2002, they were F-GZCC (c/n 448), F-GZCD (c/n 458), F-GZCE (c/n 465), F-GZCF (c/n 481), F-GZCG (c/n 498), F-GZCH (c/n 500), F-GZCI (c/n 502) and F-GZCJ (c/n 503) with their deliveries taking place on 29 January, 19 March, 28 March, 28 June, 22 November, 18 October, 20 December and 22 November respectively.

In 2003, two more were delivered. They were F-GZCK (c/n 516) and F-GZCL (c/n 519), which were delivered on 4 and 24 March respectively. F-GZCM (c/n 567) and F-GZCN (c/n 584) were delivered on 30 January and 30 March 2004 respectively, followed by the last two, F-GZCO (c/n 657) and F-GZCP (c/n 660), delivered on 4 and 18 April 2005.

These A330s immediately replaced six A310-203s with F-GEMA (c/n 316), F-GEMB (c/n 326), F-GEMC (c/n 335), F-GEMD (c/n 355), F-GEME (c/n 369) and F-GEMG (c/n 454), which had been delivered to Air France between 27 April 1984 and 18 March 1988, and four A310-304s with F-GEMN (c/n 502), F-GEMO (c/n 504), F-GEMP (c/n 550) and F-GEMQ (c/n 551) that had been delivered to the airline in 1989, 1990 and 1991.

These A310s were all retired in 2002 and 2003 and sold to FedEx to be converted into cargo aircraft, while two of the A310-304s, which had been leased from ILFC, were placed with Eagle Aviation and Islandsflug and the other two owned by Air France (F-GEMP and F-GEMQ) were sold to the Spanish Air Force (Fuerza Aérea Española) to transport Spanish government officials and the country's royal family.

F-GZCP, the last A330-203 delivered to Air France, crashed into the sea while on a transatlantic flight from Rio de Janeiro to Paris on 1 June 2009, killing 12 crew and 216 passengers. The cause of the crash was a stall and spin caused by a co-pilot mistake. The formation of ice crystals in the pitot tube meant the indicated airspeed of the aircraft was not available to the pilots. Once the aircraft was shaken by turbulence, the inexperienced co-pilot moved the control stick too much, resulting in the aircraft entering stall and spin, and diving from the sky.

Today, the remaining 15 aircraft are still in service, with 224 seats in the cabin comprising 36 business class seats, 21 premium economy seats and 167 economy class seats. Eighty per cent of the A330 flights are from Paris to sub-Saharan Africa, while a few others are to the Middle East (Beirut and Tel Aviv), two to Southeast Asia and four to the American continent.

Some of the A330-203s received fleet names. Like other aircraft in the fleet, they are named after French towns. F-GZCB is named after Chantilly, F-GZCE is named after Colmar, F-GZCF is named after Avignon, F-GZCG is named after Saint-Nazaire while F-GZCJ to F-GZCN are named after Caen, Brest, Chenonceaux, Valençay and Laval.

F-GZCA (c/n 422) is an A330-203s. It is departing Paris Charles de Gaulle Airport for Conakry (flight AF598) on 9 August 2023. (Babak Taghvaee)

F-GZCC (c/n 458) is the third A330-203 delivered to Air France. The aircraft belongs to AAR Corporation, an aircraft leasing company. It is at Paris Charles de Gaulle Airport departing for Conakry (flight AF598) on 23 June 2023. (Babak Taghvaee)

F-GZCD (c/n 458) is the fourth A330-203 operated by Air France, which was delivered on 19 March 2023. It is owned by Carlyle Aviation Partners and operates under a long-term leasing contract. (Babak Taghvaee)

F-GZCF (c/n 481) was delivered on 28 June 2002 and has been operated by Air France under a long-term leasing contract with AerCap Holdings NV. It is at Paris Charles de Gaulle Airport, departing for Chennai (flight AF108) on 2 August 2023. (Babak Taghvaee)

F-GZCG (c/n 498) with *Saint-Nazaire* fleet name is an A330-203s operated by Air France and owned by the Air France-KLM Group. It is at Paris Charles de Gaulle Airport on 6 November 2021. (Babak Taghvaee)

F-GZCH (c/n 500) was delivered to Air France on 18 October 2002. It is departing Paris Charles de Gaulle Airport on 15 January 2021. (Babak Taghvaee)

F-GZCM (c/n 567) has been in use by Air France since 30 January 2004. It is owned by the Air France-KLM Group. It is at Paris Charles de Gaulle Airport on 26 January 2023. (Babak Taghvaee)

Left: F-GZCN (c/n 584) is one of three A330-203s operated by Air France under long-term leasing contracts. The aircraft was first flown on 13 March 2004 at Toulouse and was delivered on 30 March 2004. It is at Paris Charles de Gaulle Airport on 23 June 2023. It was towed from a maintenance hangar to the terminal prior to flight AF860 to Lomé. (Babak Taghvaee)

Below: Out of 15 A330-203s currently operated by Air France, eight are owned by the Air France-KLM Group while the others are leased on long-term contracts. F-GZCO (c/n 657), which was delivered on 4 April 2005, is one of them. It is at Charles de Gaulle Airport on 11 February 2021. (Babak Taghvaee)

The Boeing 777-328ER Fleet Since 2004

In a period of 11 years, Air France received 43 Boeing 777-328ER (Extended Range) between 2005 and 2016, turning the airline into one of its largest operators in the world. Since the retirement of Air France's Airbus A380-861 wide-body and long-haul airliners, the B777-328ERs, capable of carrying 296 to 472 passengers, are the largest passenger aircraft operating long-distance flights, particularly to Caribbean and South American countries.

The Boeing 777-328ER is an extended-range variant of the Boeing 777-300 series. Its development was announced during the Paris Air Show on 26 June 1995. The first B777-300 prototype was assembled between March and July 1997, rolled out of the factory on 8 September and logged its maiden flight on 16 October. As it was longer than the B777-200 series, it could carry 60–75 extra seats, transporting 370 passengers in tri-class cabin configuration and 451 in two-class cabin configuration, or up to 550 in all-economy class cabin.

The 10.1m (33ft) extra length is formed with 5.3m (17ft) in ten frames forward and 4.8m (16ft) in nine frames aft for a 73.8m (242ft) length. The B777-300 had the fuel tanks and capacity of the B777-200ER but due to its increased weight could not increase the range of the B777-200ER.

To meet the need for a B777-300 with a higher range and maximum take-off weight, Boeing developed the B777-300ER. Thanks to its increased maximum take-off weight, it could carry more fuel, allowing a maximum range of 13,650km (7,370 n/mi/8,480 miles) with 396 passengers in a two-class seating arrangement.

The maximum take-off weight of the B777-300ER is 351,533kg (775,000lb) and the fuel tanks carry a maximum 181,283 litres (47,890 US gallons) of fuel. The maximum take-off weight of the B777-300 is 299,370kg (660,000lb) with a maximum fuel capacity of 171,171 litres (45,220 US gallons) like the B777-200ER. The B777-300ER is equipped with extended wingtips, a strengthened fuselage and wings and a modified and strengthened main landing gear due to its increased maximum take-off weight.

Being equipped with only two engines with an operating cost of almost half of the Boeing 747-400 and Airbus A340-300/500/600 wide-body passenger aircraft, the aircraft became popular with other airlines as a replacement for their ageing Boeing 747s and Airbus A340s. Air France, which had retired the majority of its old Airbus A340-211/311/312s and replaced them with Airbus A330-203s and Boeing 777-228ERs between 1997 and 2002, selected the Boeing 777-300ER as a replacement for its remaining A340-300 series as well as the four-engined Boeing 747-300 and 400 series wide-body passenger aircraft still in its service.

Kawasaki started delivery of fuselage panels for Boeing's new B777-300ER aircraft in July 2002. Assembly and production of the first B777-300ER was finished in early 2003, with its maiden flight logged on 24 February of that year. It took off at 10am Pacific time from Paine Field in Everett, WA. After flying a little over three hours, it landed at 1.02pm at Seattle's Boeing Field. Air France became its launch customer, placing an order for 16 and receiving the first of them on 29 April 2004 and 13 May. Of the order, ten were to be owned by the airline, while the remaining six were acquired on lease.

The new aircraft boasts the longest operating range. It is also larger and equipped with two General Electric GE90-115B turbofan engines that offer more power than those of its predecessor, for increased passenger capacity and greater cargo lift: 310 passengers and almost 24 tonnes of cargo. On the B777-300ER, and as of 2005 on the –200ER, Air France offered its customers the new l'Espace Première, featuring 50 per cent more personal space.

The aircraft procured by Air France received B777-328ER name designation by order of the airline; their GE90-115B turbofan engines each produced 115,540lbf (513.9kN) take-off thrust while the GE90-94B turbofans of Boeing 777-228ERs each produced 97,300lbf (432.8kN) take-off thrust.

Delivery of the Boeing 777-328ERs

The first two B777-328ERs of Air France were delivered in 2004. They were F-GSQA (c/n 32723/466) and F-GSQB (c/n 32724/478), which had been first flown on 10 January and 5 May 2004. In that year, Air France received five more, which were F-GSQC (c/n 32727/480) on 1 June; F-GSQD (c/n 32726/490) on 21 September; F-GSQE (c/n 32851/492) on 8 October; F-GSQF (c/n 32849/494) on 12 November; and F-GSQG (c/n 32850/500) on 23 December.

In 2005, four more were delivered, which were F-GSQH (c/n 32711/501) on 18 February; F-GSQI (c/n 32725/502) on 18 March; F-GSQJ (c/n 32852/510) on 29 April; and F-GSQK (c/n 32845/530) on 17 November, while in 2006, six more were delivered, which were F-GSQL (c/n 32853/545) on 13 February; F-GSQM (c/n 32848/558) on 31 March; F-GSQN (c/n 32960/565) on 30 May; F-GSQO (c/n 32961/570) on 14 June; F-GSQP (c/n 35676/573) on 30 June; and F-GSQR (c/n 35677/579) on 3 August.

In 2007, Air France received seven B777-328ERs, which were F-GSQS (c/n 32962/608) on 22 January; F-GSQT (c/n 32846/616) on 27 February; F-GSQU (c/n 32847/624) on 19 April; F-GSQV (c/n 32854/636) on 25 May; F-GSQX (c/n 32963/645) on 29 June; F-GSQY (c/n 35678/647) on 10 July; and F-GZNA (c/n 35297/671) on 24 October.

Between 2008 and 2010, Air France received seven more aircraft, which were F-GZNB (c/n 32964/715) on 2 May 2008; F-GZNC (c/n 35542/723) on 30 May 2008; F-GZND (c/n 35543/777) on 10 April 2009; F-GZNE (c/n 37432/790) on 10 June 2009; F-GZNF (c/n 37433/792) on 23 June 2009; F-GZNG (c/n 32968/795) on 26 June 2009; and F-GZNH (c/n 35544/905) on 9 December 2010.

The last group of 12 B777-328ERs were delivered to Air France between 2011 and 2016. They were F-GZNI (c/n 39973/924) on 1 April 2011; F-GZNJ (c/n 38706/928) on 15 April 2011; F-GZNK (c/n 39971/931) on 3 May 2011; F-GZNL (c/n 40063/1001) on 3 April 2012; F-GZNN (c/n 40376/1013) on 15 May 2012; F-GZNO (c/n 38665/1007) on 11 April 2012; F-GZNP (c/n 37435/1290) on 23 April 2015; F-GZNQ (c/n 40064/1298) on 6 May 2015; F-GZNR (c/n 4453/1343) on 2 November 2015; F-GZNS (c/n 39970/1380) on 9 March 2016; F-GZNT (c/n 38705/1385) on 29 March 2016; and F-GZNU (c/n 61701/1393) on 25 April 2016.

The first two B777-328ERs were a pair of Boeing 747-3B3M classic jumbo jets that had been in use by the airline since 29 December 1992 and 10 January 1991. These two aircraft, F-GETA (c/n 23413/632) and F-GETB (c/n 23480/641), were each equipped with four General Electric CF6-50E2 turbofan engines and had been built in 1986. They were in use with Union de Transport Aerien (UTA) before Air France operated them. F-GETA was withdrawn from service on 24 August 2006, while F-GETB was withdrawn from service on 12 August 2006. In August 2007, they were purchased by Blue Sky Airlines, owned by Iran's Mahan Air, which was based in Armenia. Blue Sky transferred them to Mahan Air in 2008.

Three years after the retirement of the Boeing 747-3B3Ms, Air France began replacing its Boeing 747-428 wide-body passenger aircraft manufactured in 1991 and 1992. In 2009, F-GITC (c/n 25344/889) was retired, and in 2010 F-GITA (c/n 24969/836) and F-GITB (c/n 24990/843) were withdrawn from service on 10 September and 18 October. In 2015, F-GITF (c/n 25602/909), F-GITH (c/n 32868/1325) and F-GITI (c/n 32869/1327) were retired on 10 February, 22 October and 1 November. In 2016, the last Boeing 747-428s were retired. They were F-GITD (c/n 25600/901) on 9 January, while F-GITE (c/n 25601/906) and F-GITJ (c/n 32871/1343) were retired on 11 January.

With the exception of F-GITC, which was retired in May 2009, and had 477 passenger seats (17 business, 60 premium economy and 400 economy seats), the rest of the fleet had 432 passenger seats (36 business class seats and 396 economy seats).

Current Disposition of the Fleet

Depending on the route and destinations, the Boeing 777-328ERs have four cabin configurations. The first, with 296 seats (58 business seats, 28 premium economy seats and 210 economy seats); the second with 369 seats (56 business seats, 48 premium economy seats and 265 economy seats); the third with 381 seats (42 business class seats, 24 premium economy seats and 315 economy seats); and the fourth with 472 seats (14 business seats, 28 premium economy and 430 economy seats).

Eighteen of the Boeing 777-328ERs are named after French towns: F-GSQA *Lunéville*, F-GSQB *Cheverny*, F-GSQC *Amboise*, F-GSQD *Ecouen*, F-GSQF *Papeete*, F-GSQI *Rambouillet*, F-GSQJ *Strasbourg*, F-GSQK *Amiens*, F-GSQL *Azay-Le-Rideau*, F-GSQM *Troyes*, F-GSQN *Limoges*, F-GSQO *Vezelay*, F-GSQR *Châteauroux*, F-GZND *La Rochelle*, F-GZNG *Belfort*, F-GZNH *Mulhouse*, F-GZNI *Blois* and F-GZNK *Fontainebleau*. Two other aircraft are also painted in SkyTeam colours, and these are F-GZNE and F-GZNT.

As of August 2023, Air France's B777-338ERs were flying to Washington, Atlanta, Boston, Chicago, Detroit, Denver, Los Angeles, New York, Miami, Orlando and San Francisco in the US; Shanghai and Xiamen in China; Abidjan in Côte d'Ivoire; Brazzaville in Congo; Kinshasa in DR Congo; Mumbai in India; Seoul in South Korea; Tokyo in Japan; Nairobi in Kenya; Conakry in Guinea; Bamako in Mali; Fort-de-France in Martinique; Cancún and Mexico City in Mexico; Dubai in UAE; Montreal, Toronto and Saint John's in Canada; Rio de Janeiro and Sao Paolo in Brazil; Changi Airport of Singapore; Dakar in Senegal; Nassau in Bahamas; Cotonou in Benin; Pointe-a-Pitre in Guadeloupe; Port Louis in Mauritius; Saint-Denis in Reunion; Lima in Peru; Havana in Cuba; Nouakchott in Mauritania; Yerevan in Armenia; Johannesburg in South Africa; and Bastia in Corsica.

Among the 43 Boeing 777-328ERs of the airline, 22 are owned by Air France while 21 are leased. The leased aircraft are F-GSQA, F-GSQB, F-GSQG, F-GSQH, F-GSQI, F-GSQJ, F-GSQP, F-GSQR, F-GSQX, F-GZNA, F-GZNB, F-GZNC, F-GZNE, F-GZNF, F-GZNG, F-GZNH, F-GZNI, F-GZNL, F-GZNO, F-GZNP and F-GZNR.

Boeing 777-328ER (F-GSQA (c/n 32723) named *Lunéville* taking off from Paris Charles de Gaulle Airport for a flight to Miami (flight AF90) on 2 August 2023. The aircraft is owned by AerCap Holdings NV, a leasing company. (Babak Taghvaee)

F-GSQC (c/n 32727) is a B777-328ER that has been in use by Air France since 1 June 2004. The aircraft, with *Amboise* fleet name, is at Paris Charles de Gaulle Airport on 21 September 2020. (Babak Taghvaee)

Delivered on 12 November 2004, F-GSQF (c/n 32849) is a B777-328ERs. It is at Paris Charles de Gaulle Airport on 15 January 2021. (Babak Taghvaee)

F-GSQH (c/n 32711) belongs to AerCap Holdings NV and has been in use by Air France since 2005. It is at Paris Charles de Gaulle Airport on 23 June 2023 with flight AF72 to Los Angeles. (Babak Taghvaee)

F-GSQK (c/n 32845) was delivered to Air France on 17 November 2005. The aircraft, which was first flown on 11 August 2005, was used by Boeing as a test bed for upgrades for several months before its delivery to Air France at Boeing Everett. The aircraft is departing Paris Charles de Gaulle Airport with flight AF72 to Los Angeles on 2 August 2023. (Babak Taghvaee)

Above: Delivered on 13 February 2006, F-GSQL (c/n 32853) is a B777-328ERs and is landing at Paris Charles de Gaulle Airport with flight AF459 from São Paulo on 9 August 2023. (Babak Taghvaee)

Left: Named *Troyes*, F-GSQM is one of the B777-328ERs owned by Air France, and was delivered on 31 March 2006. It is landing at Paris Charles de Gaulle Airport on 21 September 2020. (Babak Taghvaee)

Below: F-GSQR (c/n 35677) was delivered to Air France on 3 August 2006. It is departing Paris Charles de Gaulle Airport for Montreal with flight AF342 on 2 August 2023. (Babak Taghvaee)

Above: F-GSQU (c/n 32847) was delivered to Air France on 19 April 2007. It is departing Paris Charles de Gaulle Airport on 15 January 2021. (Babak Taghvaee)

Right: F-GSQY (c/n 35678) has been operated by Air France since 2007. It is departing Paris Charles de Gaulle Airport with flight AF16 to New York on 23 June 2023. (Babak Taghvaee)

Below: On 2 May 2008, F-GZNB (c/n 32964) was delivered to Air France. It was the 50th Boeing 777 for the airline. It is arriving at Paris Charles de Gaulle Airport with flight AF459 from São Paulo on 2 August 2023. (Babak Taghvaee)

F-GZNE (c/n 37432) is one of three B777-328ERs in SkyTeam Alliance colours. The aircraft is taking off from runway 26R at Charles de Gaulle Airport with flight AF178 to Mexico City on 2 August 2023. Another B777-328ER is landing on the 27R runway. (Babak Taghvaee)

F-GZNH (c/n 35544) named *Mulhouse* was delivered to Air France on 9 December 2010. It is taking off from Paris Charles de Gaulle Airport with flight AF682 to Atlanta. (Babak Taghvaee)

F-GZNI (c/n 39973) is a B777-328ERs operated under a long-term leasing contract. This example belongs to JP Lease and has been operated by the airline since 1 April 2011. It is at Paris Charles de Gaulle Airport on 11 February 2021. (Babak Taghvaee)

F-GZNK (c/n 39971) is a B777-328ER named *Fontainebleau* and operated by Air France since 3 May 2011. The aircraft was stored at Bordeaux between 27 March 2022 and 19 January 2023. It then went into commercial use (flight AF22 to New York). This image shows F-GZNK at Paris Charles de Gaulle Airport being towed to one of the terminals from the technical and maintenance facility on 23 June 2023. The aircraft flew to Saint-Denis (flight AF652) that day.

F-GZNL (c/n 40063) is owned by Air Lease Corporation and has been operated by Air France under a long-term leasing contract since 3 April 2012. It is landing at Paris Charles de Gaulle Airport following flight AF809 from Fort-de-France on 9 August 2023.

F-GZNN (c/n 40376) is one of three Air France B777-328ERs painted in SkyTeam Alliance colours. The aircraft is departing Charles de Gaulle Airport with flight AF342 to Montreal on 23 June 2023.

F-GZNO (c/n 38665) has been operated by Air France since 11 April 2012 and is on Runway 25 at Paris-Orly Airport on 22 July 2023 with flight AF671 from Saint-Denis. (Babak Taghvaee)

F-GZNT (c/n 38705), the third Air France B777-328ER painted in SkyTeam Alliance colours, is taking off from Charles de Gaulle Airport on 2 August 2023 with flight AF442 to Rio de Janeiro. (Babak Taghvaee)

The Boeing 777-F28 Fleet Since 2009

Air France's Boeing 777-F28 wide-body long-haul cargo aircraft are based on the Boeing 777-200LR (Long Range) wide-body passenger aircraft. The aircraft is capable of carrying a maximum 103,700kg (228,700lb) and can fly to a maximum range of 18,057km (9,750nmi/11,220 miles) or 9,200 km (4,970nmi/5,720 miles) at its maximum structural payload.

Boeing designed and developed the 777-200F or 777F (Freighter) as a replacement for the cargo Boeing 747-200Fs, McDonnell Douglas DC-10s, and McDonnell Douglas MD-11Fs. In 2005, Air France became the first airline to express interest in acquiring it as a replacement for its remaining fleet of classic Boeing 747-200F series.

In 2005, Air France had five Boeing 747-228Fs with r/c F-BPVZ, F-GCBG, F-GCBK, F-GCBL and F-GCBM and three Boeing 747-228B(SF) with r/c F-GCBD, F-GCBF and F-GCBH. Prior to that, the airline operated two Boeing 747-2B3Fs (F-GPAN and F-GBOX) and four Boeing 747-228Fs (F-BPVO, F-BPVR, F-GCBE and F-GPVV), which were replaced with Boeing 747-400F series wide-body cargo aircraft.

In 2002, Air France began operating two Boeing 747-428ERFs, r/c F-GIUA (delivered on 17 October) and F-GIUC (delivered on 19 November). On 31 March 2004, the airline received a third Boeing 747-428ERF, with r/c F-GIUD, and on 28 June 2005, the airline received another, with r/c F-GIUE. All aircraft had been leased from leasing companies and cargo airlines. In 2007, five more B747-400F series were added to the fleet. They were three Boeing 747-428(BCF)s with r/c F-GISA, F-GISB and F-GISE, a Boeing 747-481(BCF) with r/c F-GISF, a Boeing 747-428ERF with r/c F-GIUG and a Boeing 747-406ERF with r/c F-GIUF. All were operated on dry-leasing contracts.

On 26 March 2005, Jean-Claude Couturier, spokesperson for Air France at that time, announced that the airline was to procure Boeing 777Fs as a replacement for the remaining eight Boeing 747-200Fs, with a service entry date planned for 2008.

The first B777F logged its maiden flight on 14 July 2008 it lasted for almost three and half hours, during which the aircraft and its systems performed well. To that date, Boeing had secured 78 firm orders from 11 customers for the cargo aircraft, with Air France the first. On 19 February 2009, Air France received the first B777F, with r/c F-GUOC. It was actually the third B777F ordered by the airline.

The prototype, with Boeing 777-F28 name designation and c/n 32967/718, was equipped with a pair of GE90-110B1L turbofan engines. It had been ordered by Air France in March 2005 alongside three other B777-F28s. It logged its first flight as mentioned above on 14 July 2008, but remained undelivered until 30 November 2009, when Boeing finished testing the aircraft. Nine months prior, the second and third aircraft, with c/n 32965/732 and 32966/752 and r/c F-GUOB and F-GUOC, were delivered on 24 and 19 February 2009.

F-GUOA was sold by Air France to FedEx Express on 17 March 2010, leaving two Boeing 777-F28s in service. The fourth B777-F28 ordered by the airline in 2005 was not taken up. The aircraft with c/n 32969/827, which first flew on 4 November 2009 and later received F-r/c GUOD, was never delivered to Air France and instead was sold to FedEx Express.

Many of Air France's B747-200Fs that were to be replaced by B777-F28s were retired or withdrawn from use several years before the new deliveries, leaving only F-GCBL and F-GCBM in service, which were both B747-227Fs and had been in service since 23 February 1990 and 29 December 2010. Almost a year after delivery of the B777-F28s, F-GCBL and F-GCBM were retired on 26 and 28 April 2010.

In 2010, Air France also had three B747-428(BCF)s withdrawn from use. These were F-GISA, F-GUSB and F-GISE, and they were returned to their lessors on 30 June, 8 October and 8 September 2010. On 28 March and 18 April of the same year, F-GIUE, a Boeing 747-428ERF, and F-GISF, a Boeing 747-481(BCF), were also withdrawn. The remaining B747-400F series cargo aircraft (F-GIUA, F-GIUC, F-GIUD and F-GIUG) were withdrawn between 2013 and 2015 and returned to their lessors without being replaced.

To this date, Air France has continued operating only two B777-F28s (F-GUOB and F-GUOC). In August 2023, they were spotted frequently flying to Mexico City, Chicago, Dublin, Prestwick and Tokyo.

Air France planned to replace its Boeing 777-F28s with Airbus A350F full cargo aircraft. On 12 April 2022, Air France-KLM announced its decision to convert into a firm order the Letter of Intent it signed in December 2021 for the acquisition of four Airbus A350F full freighter aircraft – with purchase rights for an additional four aircraft. These aircraft will be operated by Air France and be based at Paris Charles de Gaulle Airport, the airline's global hub, equipped with a state-of-the-art 14,000sq m cargo terminal.

The Airbus A350F full freighter provides the most advanced technology and efficiency standards. Compared to previous generation aircraft, it offers 11 per cent more volume, enabling a 15 per cent reduction in fuel burn and CO_2 emissions, due to its reduced weight and efficient Rolls-Royce engines. It will therefore play a key role in shaping the future of Air France-KLM as an industry leader in sustainable air cargo transportation.

F-GUOB (c/n 32965) is one of two Air France Boeing 777-F28 cargo aircraft that have been operated by the airline since 24 February 2009 under a long-term leasing contract. This example is departing Charles de Gaulle Airport with flight AF6732, to Chicago, on 9 August 2023. (Babak Taghvaee)

F-GUOC (c/n 32966) is the second Boeing 777-F28 cargo aircraft and is landing at Paris Charles de Gaulle Airport with flight AF6739 from Chicago, on 9 August 2023. (Babak Taghvaee)

The Boeing 787-9 Fleet Since 2016

Both Air France and KLM are operators of the Boeing 787 Dreamliner wide-body passenger aircraft. Air France has ten B787-9s, while KLM has 13 B787-9s and ten B787-10s, with five more examples planned for delivery by the end of 2024 (as of August 2023). Initially, Air France planned to receive six Boeing 787-10s in addition to its current existing fleet of ten B787-9s, but decisions were made to swap the order with seven Airbus A350s already ordered by KLM at that time. In June 2019, a decision was made to reduce operational costs and increase profitability for both airlines.

The Boeing 787-9 series is the second member of the Dreamliner family. The first prototype made its maiden flight from Boeing's Paine Field facility on 17 September 2013. Keeping the same wingspan of the B787-8, the shortest and first variant of Dreamliner, the B787-9 has a strengthened fuselage 6.1m (20ft) longer than the previous model. The 6.1m (20ft) stretch was achieved by adding a 3.05m (10ft) (five-frame) extension forward and aft. The 787-8 and 787-9 have 50 per cent commonality: the wing, fuselage and systems of the 787-8 had required radical revision to achieve the payload-range goals of the 787-9.

With its longer and strengthened fuselage, it has a maximum take-off weight of 24,700kg (54,500lb), seats 259 passengers in a typical three-class arrangement, and a range greater than 14,140km (7,635nmi/8,786 miles). The aircraft was designed and developed as a replacement for the Boeing 767-300ER series and Airbus A330-300 series wide-body passenger aircraft in the market, with All Nippon Airways being its launch customer when it commenced commercial service on 7 August 2014.

For Air France, the Boeing 787-9s took the place of Airbus A340-311s with r/c F-GLZH (retired on 30 October 2016) and r/c F-GLZI (retired on 8 October 2017) as well as five A340-313s with r/c F-GLZR (retired on 30 October 2017), r/c F-FZNI (retired on 26 February 2017), r/c F-GLZS (retired on 21 May 2018), r/c F-GLZU (retired on 31 December 2018) and r/c F-GZLJ (retired on 1 July 2019).

At 9am local time, on Friday 2 December 2016, Air France welcomed its Boeing 787 with a water salute performed by the firefighters at Charles de Gaulle Airport. Franck Terner, Chief Executive Officer of Air France at that time declared: *'It is with pride and honour that Air France today takes delivery of its first Boeing 787, the ninth of the Air France-KLM Group. The Boeing 787 marks a new step in the modernisation of our fleet and will offer the best Air France products to our customers.'*

According to Boeing, the aircraft offered many operational advantages including saving 20 per cent fuel consumption and subsequently 20 per cent less CO_2 emissions and noise emissions.

On the occasion of the delivery of the new aircraft, Air France had four inaugural flights. They were flight AF787 to Corsica and the Mediterranean, and flight AF789 Southwest – Gascony on 7 January 2017. On 8 January, flight AF787 was to Brittany, and flight AF789 was a tour of France. The Air France Boeing 787 made its first commercial flight to Cairo on 9 January 2017. The aircraft left Paris at 14:30 local time and arrived in Cairo at 20:00 local time, with flight AF570. It departed Cairo at 01:35am, returning to Paris at 05:30am local time with flight AF567 on 10 January.

F-HRBA, Air France's first B787-9 was delivered in Seattle on 29 November 2016, three days before its flight to Charles de Gaulle Airport. The aircraft with c/n 38769 was the 500th Dreamliner to be manufactured by Boeing, and had first flown on 18 November 2016. The second aircraft with c/n 42495 and r/c F-HRBB had its first flight logged on 15 March 2017, followed by its handover to the airline on 18 April of the same year. The aircraft became the first Air France Dreamliner to fly transatlantic from Charles de Gaulle Airport to Montreal, Canada, on 1 May 2017.

In 2017, Air France received three more B787-9s with r/c F-HRBC, F-HRBD and F-HRBE on 26 September, 13 and 21 November respectively. In 2018, two more with r/cs F-HRBF and F-HRBG were delivered on 5 April and 30 November. In 2019, F-HRBH and F-HRBI were delivered on 24 April and 17 May, while on 23 July 2020, r/c F-HRBJ was delivered. The aircraft was later named *Saint Emilion*, after a commune in south-west France.

In less than 24 hours, the first Dreamliner encountered two technical issues resulting in emergency landing requests by its pilots on 10 and 11 February 2023. The first occurred during flight AF864 to Cape Town, South Africa, when the pilot had to return to Charles de Gaulle Airport only 23 minutes after take-off. The second emergency landing occurred during a flight to Malé in the Maldives. Around 20 minutes after take-off from Paris, the pilot declared an emergency and began returning to Paris. Both emergencies were due to technical failure in one of the two General Electric GEnx-1B turbofan engines. The B787-8 uses a pair of -1B70 variants of the engine, which has 69,800lbf (310kN) take-off thrust.

Air France has not received any other B787-9s or the lengthened B787-10s. Its order for six B787-10s was transferred to KLM in exchange for A350s ordered by the airline. Air France has ten B787-9s, which fly to Bangkok, Beijing, Beirut, Casablanca, Chicago, Delhi, Dallas, Dar-es-Salaam, Hong Kong, Mexico City, Montreal, Quebec, Seattle, Nairobi, Toronto and Zanzibar. They are configured with a tri-class cabin carrying a total of 279 passengers with 30 business class seats, 21 premium economy seats and 225 economy class seats.

After delivery of the nine B787-9s, Air France continued operating four A340-313s. These were withdrawn from service during the Covid-19 pandemic. They were F-GLZK, F-GLZN, F-GLZO and F-GLZP and were retired from service on 23 March, 19 March, 24 February and 23 June 2020 respectively. F-GLZK and F-GLZN were sold to Kam Air and Air X Charter. The other two were scrapped. Among the ten B787-9s of Air France, seven are known to be owned by Air France-KLM Group, while three (F-HRBA, F-HRBC and F-HRBD) are leased under long-term contracts.

F-HRBA (c/n 38769) is the first Boeing 787-9 and was delivered on 29 November 2016. The aircraft belongs to AerCap Holdings NV and has been operated by Air France under a long-term leasing contract. It is at Charles de Gaulle Airport on 6 November 2021. (Babak Taghvaee)

F-HRBB (c/n 42495) is the second Air France Boeing 787-9 and was delivered on 18 April 2017. It is one of the seven aircraft of this type owned by the Air France-KLM Group. It is at Charles de Gaulle Airport on 5 February 2021. (Babak Taghvaee)

This image taken at Paris Charles de Gaulle Airport on 25 December 2020 shows F-HRBH (c/n 42498), the eighth B787-9 departing from runway 26R. (Babak Taghvaee)

F-HRBI (c/n 42493) is the ninth Air France B787-9, which was delivered on 17 May 2019. It is at Charles de Gaulle Airport on 11 February 2021. (Babak Taghvaee)

The tenth and last Air France B787-9 with r/c F-HRBJ (c/n 42497) is departing runway 26R, Charles de Gaulle Airport, with flight AF386 to Toronto on 9 August 2023. (Babak Taghvaee)

The Airbus A350-941 Fleet Since 2019

Since 2019, Air France has operated Airbus A350-941 long-range, wide-body twin-engine jet airliners, an aircraft that was acquired to be operated alongside Boeing 787-9 for long-range and high demand routes and destinations. It was operated as a replacement for the four-engined Airbus A380-861 wide-body airliners despite carrying fewer passengers. When this book was written, the airline had 21 A350-941s in its service and was waiting for delivery of seven more by the end of 2024.

The A350 was designed and developed by Airbus in 2004 as a response to the Boeing 787 Dreamliner. It was a development of a successful A330 wide-body airliner but with composite wings and new engines. The project for design and development of the aircraft began under the name of 'XWB', which stood for (eXtra Wide Body), an aircraft that was planned to be powered by two Rolls-Royce Trent XWB high bypass turbofan engines.

On 6 October 2005, the programme's industrial launch was announced at an estimated cost of almost €3.5 billion. Based on the A330's design, it was planned initially to be a 250–300-seat wide-body aircraft using mostly aluminium-lithium alloys instead of carbon fibre-reinforced polymer (CFRP) as in the fuselage of the Boeing 787. On 14 July 2006, during the Farnborough International Air Show, Airbus announced that it had redesigned the programme for the A350 XWB, drawing the attention of various airlines including Singapore Airlines, which agreed to order 20 with options for another 20.

Under the A350 XWB design, the aircraft was of a totally new design, with a wider fuselage cross-section allowing various seating configurations for a maximum capacity of 440–475 passengers. The redesigned fuselage also had composite material used in many of its parts, allowing a higher cabin pressure and humidity and lower maintenance costs. On 1 December 2006, the Airbus board of directors approved the industrial launch of the A350-800, -900 and -1000 variants.

The two-year delay caused by the design changes increased the total cost of the programme from US$5.3 billion (€5.5 billion) to approximately US$10 billion (€9.7 billion) in December 2006, increasing the price of each aircraft to almost twice the estimate and forcing Airbus to renegotiate with its buyers. Airbus later announced that the aircraft's fuselage would have composite frames on its structure, with aluminium strips for electrical continuity as a safety measure for protection against lightning strikes.

In January 2008, Thales Group of France won a US$2.9 billion (€2 billion) 20-year contract to supply avionics and navigation equipment for the A350 XWB in a competition in which Honeywell and Rockwell Collins were competitors. However, Rockwell Collins later won another competition alongside Moog Inc to supply actuators and primary flight control actuation for the horizontal stabiliser of the aircraft.

Construction of the first static and flying prototypes of the A350 began in December 2009. Subsequently, construction of the first fuselage barrel of the aircraft, centre wingbox, and rudder began in France, Spain and China in December 2010, August 2010 and January 2011. The first forward fuselage of the aircraft was completed and delivered to the final assembly plant in Toulouse on 29 December 2011. The first A350 static model was tested on 5 April 2012 while the first prototype of the aircraft was completed in December 2012.

The A350 prototype flew for the first time from Toulouse-Blagnac Airport during a test flight lasting four hours, on 14 June 2013. It was powered by Rolls-Royce Trent XWB engines, the first prototypes of which were completed in 2010. After almost a year of tests, the aircraft received type certification from the EASA on 30 September 2014. The A350-900 was the initial version of the aircraft to enter the production line. Qatar Airways, as its launch customer, received its first aircraft on 22 December 2014. The aircraft logged its first commercial flight on 15 January 2015 between Doha and Frankfurt.

Production of the first A350-1000 prototype was completed and its first flight logged on 24 November 2016. Qatar Airways was a launch operator of the stretched variant of A350. On 20 February 2018, it received its first, which was put into commercial service on 24 February 2018, when it flew from Doha to London.

Order and Deliveries to Air France

During the Paris Air Show in June 2013, Air France-KLM Group confirmed an order for 25 Airbus A350s. This order was later increased to 28. Seven of these were planned to be operated by KLM while the rest were allocated to Air France. Both airlines also ordered Boeing 787-9, the key competitor of the Airbus A350-900 series. In June 2019, decisions were made by the group to transfer the seven A350s ordered for KLM to Air France in exchange for six Boeing 787s that KLM was to receive.

In 2019, Air France received its first three A350-941s, which were powered by Rolls-Royce Trent XWB-84 turbofan engines, each producing 84,200lbf (375kN) take-off thrust. The aircraft, with c/n 331, 349 and 359, flew for the first time on 27 August, 5 October and 12 November 2019 as F-HTYA, F-HTYB and F-HTYC, respectively. They were rolled out of the Airbus delivery centre on 18 September, 29 October and 30 November 2019.

After completion of the test flights, the first Air France A350-941 flew to Charles de Gaulle Airport on 27 September 2019 after an official handover ceremony in Toulouse. It was put into commercial use on 7 October 2023 and, together with the two other A350s delivered that year, it was gradually deployed to six destinations. The first Airbus A350 was named *Toulouse* by Anne-Marie Couderc, Chair of Air France-KLM and Air France, and the aircraft's sponsor at that time.

The Airbus A350 consumes 25 per cent less fuel (2.5 litres per passenger per 100km) than the Airbus A380 due to the incorporation of materials which are up to 67 per cent lighter (53 per cent composites and 14 per cent titanium). In addition, its noise footprint is reduced by 40 per cent. Passengers could also enjoy a more spacious cabin and 30 per cent larger windows than the A380; a different air pressure system provides a more comfortable cabin atmosphere with regularly renewed cabin air; and lighting adapts to the different flight phases.

The A350s flew to Abidjan, Ivory Coast, from 7 October 2019 to 8 December 2019, and from 10 February 2020 for the summer season that year; followed by Bamako in Mali from 7 October 2019 to 8 December 2019, and from 10 February 2020 for the 2020 summer season; Toronto in Canada from 27 October 2019; Cairo in Egypt from 9 December 2019, Seoul in South Korea from 9 December 2019; and Bangkok in Thailand from summer 2020.

In 2020, Air France received three more aircraft, which were F-HTYD (c/n 381) on 4 February, F-HTYE (c/n 407) on 12 June and F-HTYF (c/n 422) on 3 June. They were first flown at Toulouse on 14 January, 10 April and 3 June, respectively.

Deliveries speeded up in 2021, seven more arriving: F-HTYG (c/n 479), F-HTYH (c/n 488), F-HTYI (c/n 491), F-HTYJ (c/n 500), F-HTYK (c/n 502), F-HTYL (c/n 510) and F-HTYM (c/n 520). They first flew on 2 February, 25 February, 19 March, 18 May, 12 May, 8 July and 19 May 2021 respectively, and were rolled out of the factory for delivery on 22 March, 6 April, 26 April, 6 July, 14 June, 3 December and 20 December 2021.

Air France received seven more aircraft in 2022, which were F-HTYN (c/n 544), F-HTYO (c/n 546), F-HTYP (c/n 548), F-HTYQ (c/n 551), F-HTYR (c/n 562), F-HTYS (c/n 576) and F-HTYT (c/n 578). They were first flown at Toulouse on 13 December 2021, 27 January 2022, 6 April 2022, 4 May 2022, 23 June 2022, 30 September 2022, and 18 November 2022, respectively, with their deliveries taking place on 27 January, 11 March, 6 April, 4 May, 23 June, 30 September and 18 November 2022. In 2023, the 21st A350 with r/c F-HUVA (c/n 603) was delivered to Air France on 8 July. It had first flown at Toulouse on 6 June 2023. Its ferry flight from Toulouse to Charles de Gaulle Airport took place on 18 July 2023.

In August 2023, three of the seven remaining Air France A350s, originally ordered for KLM then swapped for Boeing 787s in June 2019, were manufactured and passed their tests at Toulouse. They were F-HUVB, F-HUVC and F-HUVD. A fourth aircraft with r/c F-HUVE was completed but had not yet received engines. Three more were in various stages of construction, with at least one on the final assembly lines. Deliveries of these aircraft were scheduled to take place in 2023 and 2024.

Current Status of the A350 Fleet

All Air France A350s are named after various communities or towns in France. The aircraft with r/c F-HTYA to F-HTYT are named after Toulouse, Lyon, Saint-Denis de La Reunion, Nice, Bordeaux, Marseille, Reims, Dijon, Saint-Malo, Cannes, Aubusson, Pointe-à-Pitre, Fort-de-France, Chambord, Cayenne, Lille, Menton, Deauville, Biscarrosse and Angers. The F-HUVA to F-HUVE were named after Aix-en-Provence, Les Sables d'Olonne, Le Havre, Nantes and Orléans.

Among the aircraft currently in use, 11 have long-term leasing contracts. These are F-HTYG, F-HTYH, F-HTYI, F-HTYJ, F-HTYM, F-HTYN, F-HTYO, F-HTYP, F-HTYR, F-HTYS, F-HTYT and F-HUVA. Of the seven remaining aircraft, at least one will be operated with a long-term leasing contract.

Following restrictions on air travel during the Covid-19 pandemic, Air France's fleet of Airbus A380-861s were put into storage at Charles de Gaulle Airport in late 2019 and early 2020. The aircraft were six to 11 years old and were withdrawn from use in 2020. They were sold to Tarmac Aerosave, which scrapped four of them between 2021 and 2023.

In total, the ten Air France A380-861s were: F-HPJA (c/n 33 in service from 30 October 2009 to 22 March 2020; F-HPJB (c/n 40) from 10 February 2010 to 31 December 2019; F-HPJC (c/n 43) from 14 April 2010 to 26 February 2020; F-HPJD (c/n 49) from 12 August 2010 to 22 March 2020; F-HPJE (c/n 52) from 17 May 2011 to 22 March 2020; F-HPJG (c/n 67) from 4 June 2012 to 13 March 2020; F-HPJH (c/n 99) from 2 May 2012 to 22 March 2020; F-HPJI (c/n 115) from 13 September 2013 to 20 March 2020; and F-HPJJ (c/n 117) from 23 June 2014 to 21 March 2020.

Replacing them in service were Air France's A350-941s despite carrying maximum 324 passengers (192 less than the A380). Today, Air France's A350-941s have two types of passenger seating configuration: one with 292 seats (48 business class, 32 premium economy class and 212 economy class), and the other with 324 seats (34 business class, 24 premium economy and 266 economy class).

F-HTYA (c/n 331) was the first Air France A350-941 and flew for the first time on 27 August 2019. It was delivered on 18 September 2019. The aircraft, named *Toulouse,* **is landing at Charles de Gaulle Airport on runway 26L with flight AF321 from Boston on 9 August 2023. (Babak Taghvaee)**

F-HTYB (c/n 349) is the second Air France A350-941, which was delivered on 29 October 2019. The aircraft is at Charles de Gaulle Airport on 15 January 2023. (Babak Taghvaee)

F-HTYH (c/n 488) named *Dijon* first flew on 25 February 2021 and was handed over to Air France on 6 April 2021. It is at Charles de Gaulle Airport on 18 April 2021. (Babak Taghvaee)

A350-941 with r/c F-HTYJ (c/n 500) departs Charles de Gaulle Airport with flight AF182 to Singapore on 2 August 2023. (Babak Taghvaee)

Left: F-HTYM (c/n 520) named *Fort-de-France* was delivered to Air France on 20 October 2021. It is arriving at Charles de Gaulle Airport with flight AF292 from Osaka on 9 August 2023. (Babak Taghvaee)

Below: An Air France A350-941 with r/c F-HTYP (c/n 548) departs Charles de Gaulle Airport with flight AF356 to Toronto on 23 June 2023. The aircraft named *Lille* was on 6 April 2022. (Babak Taghvaee)

F-HTYR (c/n 562) was delivered to Air France on 4 May 2022 and named *Deauville*. It is arriving at Charles de Gaulle Airport with flight AF935 from Antananarivo, Madagascar, on 9 August 2023. (Babak Taghvaee)

F-HPJA (c/n 33) was the first of ten Air France A380s. It flew on 12 February 2009 for the first time and was delivered on 30 October 2009. The aircraft logged its last commercial flight from Mexico City to Charles de Gaulle Airport on 22 March 2009 and was later flown to Tarbes on 18 August 2020 where it was put into storage. This aircraft is at London Heathrow on 13 June 2010. (Chris Lofting)

Air France Airbus A380-861 with r/c F-HPJD (c/n 49) prior to delivery and still wearing the temporary r/c F-WWAL in the factory. F-HPJD began its commercial service in August 2010 and was withdrawn from service on 22 February 2022, almost two years after it had been put into storage on 22 March 2020. It was later scrapped at Tarbes. (EZ/ZX Collection)

Chapter 3
The Regional Jets Fleet

The Embraer ERJ-170 Fleet Since 2019

In 2001, Air France-KLM Group established a subsidiary company to undertake regional flights from France. The airline named Régional or Regional Compagnie Aerienne had a network serving most French cities and a large number of European cities. Its head office was located in Nantes Atlantique Airport, in the town of Bouguenais and it had two maintenance sites in Clermont-Ferrand and Lille. Its aircraft had the Air France by Régional logo on their fuselages. The aircraft transported four million passengers in 2009.

On 31 March 2013, Régional and two other regional companies of the Air France-KLM Group named Airlinair and Brit Air merged and formed Hop! At the time of its merger, Régional had 23 Embraer ERJ-145s, 16 ERJ-170s and ten ERJ-190s, which could carry 50, 76 and 100 passengers respectively.

In March 2013, Brit Air had nine Bombardier CRJ-100ER (CL-600-2B19s), each with 50 economy seats, 21 Bombardier CRJ-701 (CL-600-2C10)s each with 70 economy seats, 13 Bombardier CRJ-1000EL (CL-600-2E25) each with 100 economy seats. The 13 CRJ-1000ELs had replaced 13 Fokker 100s, which the airline had withdrawn from service between 2009 and 2011. Airlinair, the other airline, which was merged with Régional, had 13 ATR-42-500s, each with 48 economy seats, two Cargo ATR 72-202(QC)s and eight ATR 72-500 (72-212As), each with 70 passenger seats at the time of its merger.

Hop! was renamed Air France Hop on 1 February 2019 and provided Air France-KLM Group with the means for countering the loss of market share to low-cost airlines in short- and medium-haul flights. From 2008, regional airlines in the group had encountered losses as low-cost airlines such as Ryan Air absorbed many of their passengers. Hop! was officially inaugurated on 26 March 2013 during a ceremony at Paris-Orly Airport in the presence of Air France CEO Alexandre de Juniac as well as Minister Delegate for Transport Frédéric Cuvillier. On 31 March 2013, the new airline saw its first flight, linking Paris-Orly to Perpignan using a Bombardier CRJ-1000 inherited from Brit Air.

Air France Hop inherited five ERJ170LR (Long Range) aircraft and 11 RJ170STD (Standard) from Régional with r/c F-HBXA to F-HBXP inclusive, which had been delivered between 28 August 2008 and 9 July 2012. Among these, six (with r/c F-HBXK to F-HBXP) had long-term leasing contracts.

ERJ170 is the smallest member of Embraer's E-Jet family of narrow-body, short- to medium-range, twin-engined jet airliners designed and produced by Brazilian aerospace manufacturer Embraer. The aircraft's development dates back to the early 1990s, with the first prototype performing its maiden flight on 19 February 2002. A total of six prototypes were manufactured, which were used over several years of test programmes. ERJ170 was the first to enter service in March 2004.

The ERJ170 is equipped with a pair of General Electric CF34-8E5 turbofan engines, each producing 14,200lb (62.28kN) of thrust and can carry 72–78 passengers in low and high density configurations. With Air France Hop, the aircraft has 76 passenger seats, comprising 20 premium economy seats and 56 economy seats.

Out of the 16 inherited ERJ170s, the three with r/c F-HBXK, F-HBXO and F-HBXP were returned to their lessors GECAS and AerCap Holdings NV on 21 April 2022, 17 June 2022 and September 2016. This left Air France Hop with ten ERJ170STDs with r/c F-HXBA–F-HBXJ and three ERJ170LRs with r/c F-HBXL, F-HBXM and F-HBXN in service. Among these, F-HBXB, F-HBXF, F-HBXG, F-HBXI and F-HBXJ received Air France's paint scheme while the rest were still in Hop! colours when this book was written in August 2023.

Air France Hop operates ten ERJ170STD (Standard), among them is the oldest – F-HBXA (c/n 17000237), which was delivered to Regional Compagnie Aerienne on 29 August 2008. It is at Charles de Gaulle Airport on 1 January 2021. (Babak Taghvaee)

Right: This Air France Hop ERJ170STD with r/c F-HBXD (c/n 17000281) was delivered to Regional Compagnie Aerienne on 10 April 2009 and transferred to Air France Hop on 31 March 2013. It is at Charles de Gaulle Airport on 20 August 2021. (Babak Taghvaee)

Below: F-HBXF (c/n 17000292) another ERJ170STD Air France Hop taking off from Charles de Gaulle Airport with flight AF9450 to Nantes on 9 August 2023. (Babak Taghvaee)

Embraer ERJ-190 Fleet Since 2019

Air France Hop's ten ERJ190s have 100 passenger seats. Registration codes F-HBLA–F-HBLJ were delivered on 22 November 2006, 18 January 2007, 10 May 2007, 27 September 2007, 25 October 2007, 27 March 2008, 18 February 2009, 26 March 2009, 16 July 2009 and 23 September 2009. Among these, four with r/cs F-HBLF–F-HBLJ are ERJ190STD (Standard), while the rest are ERJ190LR (Long Range). The ERJ190s took the place of five Fokker 70s (each with 79 passenger seats) and ten Fokker 100s (each with 109 passenger seats) in service with Régional.

The ERJ190 is a stretched variant of the ERJ170. It is fitted with a new, larger wing, a larger horizontal stabilizer, two emergency over-wing exit doors and a new more powerful engine. The ERJ190 has a pair of General Electric CF34-10E turbofan engines, rated at 18,500lbf (82.29kN). They are equipped with full authority digital engine control (FADEC). Thanks to a new computerised management system, which continuously optimizes the engine performance, it has a significantly reduced fuel consumption as well as maintenance requirements. With its powerful engines, ERJ190 can carry 100 to 124 passengers in low- and high-intensity seating arrangements.

In addition to the ten ERJ190s inherited from Régional, Air France Hop also had ten more aircraft added to its fleet. They were all ERJ190STD (Standard). The aircraft, equipped with CF34-10E5 turbofan engines, were F-HBLR (c/n 19000322), F-HBLS (c/n 19000326), F-HBLV (c/n 19000689), F-HBLK (c/n 19000760), F-HBLL (c/n 19000767), F-HBLM (c/n 19000768), F-HBLN (c/n 19000769), F-HBLO (c/n 19000770), F-HBLP (c/n 19000771) and F-HBLQ (c/n 19000773), which were delivered on 12 January 2022, 25 January 2022, 12 July 2023, 21 December 2018, 15 May 2019, 22 August 2019, 20 September 2019, 18 October 2019, 30 December 2019 and 25 September 2020.

These ERJ190s and ERJ170s connect Charles de Gaulle and Orly airports to other cities in France and fly to African and European destinations including Algiers, Amsterdam, Bilbao, Dublin, Dusseldorf, Gothenburg, Hamburg, Manchester, Olbia, Palma de Mallorca, Turin, Tunis, Venice, Vienna and Zagreb. Air France Hop connects Bordeaux, Lyon, Marseille, Nantes and Paris to international destinations.

F-HLBA (c/n 19000051) is an Air France Hop ERJ190LR aircraft taking off from Charles de Gaulle Airport with flight AF1510 to Hamburg on 23 June 2023. (Babak Taghvaee)

Above: Another ERJ190LRs with r/c F-HBLD (c/n 19000113) landing at Charles de Gaulle Airport with flight AF1095 from Cork on 2 August 2023. (Babak Taghvaee)

Right: F-HLBG (c/n 19000254) is an ERJ190STDs landing at Charles de Gaulle Airport with flight AF13515 from Birmingham on 9 August 2023. (Babak Taghvaee)

Below: F-HLBJ (c/n 19000311), another ERJ190STDs, is departing Charles de Gaulle Airport with flight AF1016 to Dublin on 9 August 2023. (Babak Taghvaee)

F-HBLM (c/n 19000768) is a new ERJ190STDs with Air France Hop since 22 August 2019. One of a few ERJ190s in the colours of Air France, it is at Charles de Gaulle Airport on 21 September 2020. (Babak Taghvaee)

F-HBLJ, an ERJ190STDs inherited by Air France Hop from Regional Compagnie Aerienne in 2013. The aircraft had been delivered on 24 September 2009. It is at Charles de Gaulle Airport with flight AF1453 from Gothenburg on 22 August 2023. (Babak Taghvaee)

F-GRZJ (c/n 10096) is a Bombardier CRJ-700/701s originally with Brit Air and inherited by Air France Hop after its formation in March 2013. This CRJ-701, which was built in 2003, was later withdrawn and sold to Skywest Airlines on 27 December 2021. It is at Zagreb on 11 April 2011, operated by Brit Air on behalf of Air France. (Chris Lofting)

Between 2000 and 2013, Air France owned all the shares of Dublin-based regional airline CityJet. During this time, it operated 48 aircraft, comprising four BAe-146-100s, 23 BAe-146-200s, six BAe-146-300s and 15 RJ85s. Of these aircraft, 23 were painted in Air France colours. EI-RJH was one of them and is at Zagreb on 3 October 2013. (Chris Lofting)

Appendix 1
Incidents and Accidents

Through its 90 years of history, Air France has experienced 141 incidents and accidents. Twelve incidents occurred before World War Two while 11 occurred during the war. The table provides details of many of these incidents and accidents.

Date	Type	Registration	C/N	Place	Crew/Passengers	Casualties
16/11/1933	Lioré et Olivier 213	F-AIFD	1	near Beauvais, France	2/0	0/0
15/01/1934	Dewoitine D.332	F-AMMY	01	Corbigny, France	3/7	3/7
31/05/1934	Lioré et Olivier 213	F-AIVG	3	Croydon, England	2/0	2/0
10/12/1935	Potez 62	F-ANPH	3845	near Auxerre, France	4/3	0/0
08/05/1936	Lioré-et-Olivier H.242/1	F-ANQG	10	near Algeria, Mediterranean Sea	3/7	0/0
27/10/1937	Dewoitine D.333	F-ANQA	01	near El Jadida, Morocco	3/3	3/3
08/12/1937	Potez 621	F-AOTZ	4213	near Saint-Sauveur, France	3/4	2/0
09/02/1938	Lioré-et-Olivier H.242/1	F-ANPB	4	Étang de Berre	5/9	2/5
07/03/1938	Potez 62	F-ANQR	4031	Datia, India	3/4	3/4
23/03/1938	Dewoitine D.338	F-AQBB	2	Cinq-Croix mountain, France	3/5	3/5
27/01/1939	Potez 62	F-ANPJ	3926	near Köln-Butzweilerhof, Germany	4/2	4/2
02/05/1939	Dewoitine D.338	F-ARIC	2	near Argana, Morocco	3/6	3/6
03/03/1940	Bloch 220	F-AOHA	1	near Orange, France	3/0	3/0
20/06/1940	Dewoitine D.338	F-ARTD	22	near Ouistreham, France	1/0	1/0
07/07/1940	Dewoitine D.338	F-AQBA	1	Gulf of Tonkin, Vietnam	4/0	4/0
10/10/1940	Dewoitine D.338	F-AQBJ	10	Carnotville, Benin	3/0	3/0
27/11/1940	SNCAC (Farman) NC.223.4	F-AROA	2	near Sardinia, Mediterranean Sea	5/2	5/2
1940	Dewoitine D.338	F-AQBH	8	Indochina	Unknown	Unknown
01/09/1941	Bloch 220	F-AQNL	12	near Marseille, France	3/14	3/12
02/07/1942	Lockheed 18-07-01 Lodestar	F-ARTL	18-2011	near Port-Étienne, Mauritania	3/0	3/0

Incidents and Accidents

Date	Type	Registration	C/N	Place	Crew/Passengers	Casualties
13/08/1942	Lioré-et-Olivier H.246.1	F-AREJ	403	Mediterranean Sea, near Algiers	3/4	0/4
27/09/1942	Dewoitine D.342	F-ARIZ	1	Ameur-el-Aïn, Algeria	7/18	7/18
13/01/1943	Lockheed 14-H2 Super Electra	F-ARRF	1506	Aguelhok, Mali	3/0	3/0
10/09/1945	Amiot AAC.1 (Junkers Ju-52)	F-BAJP	AAC019	Paris-Le Bourget, France	0/0	0/0
31/10/1945	Latécoère 631	F-BANT	2	Laguna de Rocha, Uruguay	Unknown/Unknown	0/2
10/11/1945	Amiot AAC.1 (Junkers Ju-52)	F-BANO	AAC149	Paris-Le Bourget Airport, France	0/0	0/0
23/11/1945	Amiot AAC.1 (Junkers Ju-52)	F-BAKL	AAC102	Toulouse, France	Unknown	Unknown
25/12/1945	Lockheed C-60A Lodestar	F-BALV	18-2380	near Bangui, Central African Republic	3/5	3/5
13/01/1946	Amiot AAC.1 (Junkers Ju-52)	F-BANP	AAC150	Le Bouscat, France	2/0	2/0
02/02/1946	Amiot AAC.1 (Junkers Ju-52)	F-BALK	AAC096	Belo Airport, Madagascar	0/0	0/0
04/02/1946	Amiot AAC.1 (Junkers Ju-52)	F-BAKO	AAC057	Menorca-Mahón Airport, Spain	3/16	0/0
28/06/1946	Amiot AAC.1 (Junkers Ju-52)	F-BAJS	AAC020	near Pau-Uzein Airport, France	3/0	2/0
08/08/1946	Amiot AAC.1 (Junkers Ju-52)	F-BAJT	AAC044	Paris-Le Bourget Airport, France	Unknown	Unknown
03/09/1946	Douglas DC-3A	F-BAOB	11714	near Køge, Denmark	5/17	5/17
04/09/1946	Douglas DC-3D	F-BAXD	42975	near Paris-Le Bourget Airport, France	5/21	4/19
01/02/1947	Douglas DC-3C	F-BAXQ	25251	near Lisboa-Portela de Sacavém, Portugal	5/11	5/10
05/03/1947	Amiot AAC.1 (Junkers Ju-52)	F-BAKP	AAC058	Paris-Le Bourget Airport, France	Unknown	Unknown
14/03/1947	Douglas DC-3A	F-BAXO	20488	Mount Moucherolle, France	5/18	5/18
20/03/1947	Amiot AAC.1 (Junkers Ju-52)	F-BAKM	AAC055	Freetown, Sierra Leone	Unknown	Unknown
30/04/1947	Amiot AAC.1 (Junkers Ju-52)	F-BBYG	AAC227	Niamey, Niger	Unknown	Unknown
04/06/1947	Amiot AAC.1 (Junkers Ju-52)	F-BANB	AAC136	near Gémenos, France	3/0	3/0
07/06/1947	Amiot AAC.1 (Junkers Ju-52)	F-BAKV	AAC074	Dakar-Yoff Airport, Senegal	Unknown	Unknown

Date	Type	Registration	C/N	Place	Crew/ Passengers	Casualties
01/07/1947	Amiot AAC.1 (Junkers Ju-52)	F-BALF	AAC091	near Eséka, Senegal	3/10	3/10
04/10/1947	Amiot AAC.1 (Junkers Ju-52)	F-BAJB	AAC002	Pau, France	Unknown	Unknown
07/10/1947	SNCASE SE.161 Languedoc	F-BATY	25	Bone, France	Unknown	Unknown
06/01/1948	Douglas DC-3D	F-BAXC	42972	near Gonesse, France	5/11	5/11
26/01/1948	SNCASE SE.161/ P7 Languedoc	F-BCUC	29	near Paris-Le Bourget Airport, France	9/0	9/0
04/02/1948	SNCASE SE.161/ P7 Languedoc	F-BATK	11	Marignane, Framce	0/0	0/0
10/02/1948	SNCASE SE.161/ P7 Languedoc	F-BATH	08	Paris, France	Unknown	Unknown
10/04/1948	Douglas DC-4-1009	F-BBDC	42935	Kano International Airport, Nigeria	6/0	1/0
14/06/1948	SNCASE SE.161/ P7 Languedoc	F-BATG	07	Coulommiers Airport, France	4/5	0/0
12/07/1948	Douglas DC-4-1009	F-BBDL	42989	Paris-Orly Airport, France	4/8	0/0
01/08/1948	Latécoère 631	F-BDRC	6	Atlantic Ocean	12/40	12/40
29/08/1948	SNCASE SE.161/ P7 Languedoc	F-BATO	32	Le Bourget Airport, France	0/0	0/0
23/11/1948	SNCASE SE.161/ P7 Languedoc	F-BATM	13	Toulouse, France	5/0	1/0
09/04/1949	SNCASE SE.161/ P7 Languedoc	F-BATU	23	Nice Airport, France	5/30	0/0
20/10/1949	Douglas C-54A (DC-4)	F-BBDS	10423	near Karachi Airport, Pakistan	Unknown	0/0
28/10/1949	Lockheed L-749-79-46 Constellation	F-BAZN	2546	Redondo Mountain, Portugal	11/37	11/37
28/11/1949	Douglas C-54A (DC-4)	F-BELO	10391	Saint-Just-Chaleyssin, France	5/33	4/1
22/01/1950	Douglas DC-4-1009	F-BBDB	42912	Paris-Orly Airport, France	0/0	0/0
16/02/1950	Douglas DC-3A	F-BAOD	11720	Cotonou Airport, Benin	3/0	0/0
12/06/1950	Douglas DC-4-1009	F-BBDE	42937	Persian Gulf, off Bahrain	8/44	6/40
14/06/1950	Douglas DC-4-1009	F-BBDM	42990	Persian Gulf, off Bahrain	8/45	3/37
30/07/1950	SNCASE SE.161/ P7 Languedoc	F-BCUI	30	Marseille-Marignane Airport, France	7/24	0/0
03/02/1951	Douglas DC-4-1009	F-BBDO	42992	near Buéa, Cameroon	6/23	6/23
11/08/1951	Douglas DC-3D	F-BAXB	42971	Moisville, France	5/0	5/0

Incidents and Accidents

Date	Type	Registration	C/N	Place	Crew/Passengers	Casualties
02/01/1952	Amiot AAC.1 (Ju-52)	F-BAMQ	AAC106	Andapa, Madagascar	3/8	3/3
03/03/1952	SNCASE SE.161/P7 Languedoc	F-BCUM	43	near Nice-le Var Airport, France	4/34	4/34
07/04/1952	SNCASE SE.161/P7 Languedoc	F-BATB	02	Paris-Le Bourget Airport, France	5/18	0/0
29/04/1952	Douglas C-54A (DC-4)	F-BELI	3098	near Berlin, Germany	6/11	0/0
05/12/1952	Amiot AAC.1 (Ju-52)	F-BANK	CC145	Antalaha-Antsirabato, Madagascar	0/0	0/0
10/04/1953	Amiot AAC.1 (Ju-52)	F-BALE	AAC090	Miandrivazo Airport, Madagascar	3/1	3/1
03/08/1953	Lockheed L-749A Constellation	F-BAZS	2628	Mediterranean Sea, off Fethiye, Turkey	8/34	0/4
01/09/1953	Lockheed L-749A Constellation	F-BAZZ	2674	Mont Le Cimet, France	9/33	9/33
03/08/1954	Lockheed L-1049C Super Constellation	F-BGNA	4510	Preston City, US	8/29	0/0
25/08/1954	Lockheed L-749 Constellation	F-BAZI	2513	Gander Airport, Canada	9/58	0/0
18/03/1955	Douglas C-47A (DC-3)	F-BAXL	20047	Beauvais-Tillé Airport, France	9/0	9/0
21/09/1955	Douglas C-47A (DC-3)	F-BCYU	10151	Bordeaux-Mérignac Airport, France	3/0	3/0
24/01/1956	Douglas C-47A (DC-3)	F-BAXT	9274	Nantes-Chateau Bougon Airport, France	5/0	0/0
28/01/1956	Douglas C-47A (DC-3)	F-BCYK	4509	near Lyon-Bron Airport, France	3/0	3/0
12/12/1956	Vickers 708 Viscount	F-BGNK	8	near Dannemois, France	5/0	5/0
08/04/1957	Douglas C-47B-5-DK (DC-3)	F-BEIK	25856	near Biskra Airport, Algeria	5/27	5/27
02/11/1957	Douglas C-54-DO (DC-4)	F-BHKY	3055	Toulouse Airport, France	0/0	0/0
06/12/1957	Lockheed L-1049G Super Constellation	F-BHMK	4670	Paris-Orly Airport, France	6/0	0/0
08/01/1958	Douglas DC-3A	F-BAOA	11708	Poitiers-Biard Airport, France	6/2	0/0
20/04/1958	Douglas C-54A-1-DO (DC-4)	F-BELK	7451	near In Salah Airport, Algeria	Unknown	0
31/05/1958	Douglas C-47A-85-DL (DC-3)	F-BHKV	20001	near Molière, Algeria	3/12	3/12
24/12/1958	Lockheed L-749A Constellation	F-BAZX	2527	near Wien-Schwechat Airport, Austria	6/28	0/0

Date	Type	Registration	C/N	Place	Crew/Passengers	Casualties
30/04/1959	Douglas C-47B (DC-3)	F-BAII	25550	Poitiers-Biard Airport, France	3/0	0/0
29/08/1960	Lockheed L-1049G Super Constellation	F-BHBC	4622	off Dakar-Yoff Airport, Senegal	8/55	8/55
10/05/1961	Lockheed L-1649A Starliner	F-BHBM	1027	near Edjele, Algeria	9/69	9/69
27/07/1961	Boeing 707-328	F-BHSA	17613	Hamburg-Fuhlsbüttel Airport, Germany	15/26	0/0
12/09/1961	SE-210 Caravelle III	F-BJTB	68	near Rabat-Sale Airport, Morocco	6/71	6/71
03/06/1962	Boeing 707-328	F-BHSM	17920	Paris-Orly Airport, France	10/122	8/122
22/06/1962	Boeing 707-328	F-BHST	18247	Pointe-à-Pitre-Le Raizet Airport, Guadeloupe	10/103	10/103
30/07/1962	Douglas DC-3A	F-BAOE	11769	near Coulommiers-Voisins Airport, France	8/0	5/0
26/09/1963	Douglas C-47A (DC-3)	F-BHKU	25457	Oran, Algeria	0/0	0/0
05/03/1968	Boeing 707-328C	F-BLCJ	19724	near Pointe-à-Pitre, Guadeloupe	11/52	11/52
11/09/1968	SE-210 Caravelle III	F-BOHB	244	Mediterranean Sea, off Nice	6/89	6/89
28/05/1969	Douglas C-54A (DC-4)	F-BFCP	10346	Paris-Orly Airport, France	3/0	0/0
09/09/1969	SE-210 Caravelle III	F-BHRY	61	Marseille-Marignane Airport, France	6/87	0/0
03/12/1969	Boeing 707-328B	F-BHSZ	18459	near Caracas-Simon Bolivar Airport, Venezuela	21/41	21/41
11/08/1973	Fokker F-27 Friendship 500	F-BSUM	10447	Strasbourg-Entzheim Airport, France	3/0	0/0
18/10/1973	Boeing 727-228	F-BOJC	19545	Marseille-Marignane Airport, France	12/98	0/1
24/07/1974	Fokker F-27 Friendship 500	F-BPUI	10389	near Héric, France	3/0	3/0
12/06/1975	Boeing 747-128	N28888	20542	Bombay-Santacruz Airport, India	18/376	0/0
27/06/1976	Airbus A300B4-203	F-BVGG	019	Entebbe Airport, Uganda	12/242	0/0
28/08/1976	SE-210 Caravelle III	F-BSGZ	83	Ho Chi Minh City, Vietnam	6/14	0/1
07/09/1976	Boeing 707-328	F-BHSH	17620	Ajaccio-Campo dell'Oro Airport, France	0/0	0/0

Incidents and Accidents

Date	Type	Registration	C/N	Place	Crew/ Passengers	Casualties
12/08/1977	Airbus A300	Unknown	Unknown	Brindisi-Papola Casale Airport, Italy	12/230	0/0
12/03/1979	SE-210 Caravelle III	F-BHRL	31	Frankfurt International Airport, Germany	6/35	0/0
17/03/1982	Airbus A300B4-203	F-BVGK	070	Sana'a International Airport, Yemen	13/111	0/0
27/08/1983	Boeing 727-228	Unknown	Unknown	Tehran-Mehrabad International Airport, Iran	11/100	0/0
18/01/1984	Boeing 747	Unknown	Unknown	near Karachi, Pakistan	15/246	0/0
07/03/1984	Boeing 737-228	Unknown	Unknown	Genève-Cointrin Airport, Switzerland	6/61	0/0
31/07/1984	Boeing 737-228	F-GBYH	23007	Tehran-Mehrabad International Airport, Iran	6/58	0/0
02/12/1985	Boeing 747-228B	F-GCBC	22427	Galeão Airport, Brazil	17/265	0/0
21/12/1987	Embraer EMB-120RT Brasilia	F-GEGH	120033	near Bordeaux-Mérignac, France	3/13	3/13
26/06/1988	Airbus A320-111	F-GFKC	009	Mulhouse-Habsheim Airport, France	6/130	0/3
24/07/1988	Boeing 747-228B (SCD)	N4506H	22794	Indira Gandhi International Airport, India	15/260	0/0
23/08/1989	Airbus A300B4-203	F-BVGO	129	Algiers-Houari Boumediene Airport, Algeria	11/104	0/0
12/09/1993	Boeing 747-428	F-GITA	24969	Papeete-Faaa Airport, French Polynesia	16/256	0/0
10/12/1993	Airbus A320-211	F-GFKK	100	Nice-Côte d'Azur Airport, France	6/123	0/0
20/01/1994	Airbus A340-211	F-GNIA	010	Charles de Gaulle Airport, France	0/0	0/0
26/12/1994	Airbus A300B2-1C	F-GBEC	104	Marseille-Provence Airport, France	170 in total	7
20/04/1998	Boeing 727-230	HC-BSU	21622	near Bogotá-Eldorado Airport, Colombia	10/43	10/43
12/02/1999	Airbus A320-211	F-GJVG	270	Grenouillet, France	6/163	0/0
02/03/1999	Airbus A320-211	Unknown	Unknown	Charles de Gaulle Airport, France	82 in total	0/0
04/03/1999	Boeing 737-228	F-GBYA	23000	Biarritz Parme Airport, France	6/91	0/0

Date	Type	Registration	C/N	Place	Crew/Passengers	Casualties
05/03/1999	Boeing 747-2B3F (SCD)	F-GPAN	21515	Chennai Airport, India	5/0	0/0
25/07/2000	Concorde 101	F-BTSC	203	near Charles de Gaulle Airport, France	9/100	9/100
27/02/2003	Concorde 101	F-BVFA	205	over Atlantic Ocean	6/39	0/0
02/08/2005	Airbus A340-313X	F-GLZQ	289	Toronto-Pearson International Airport, Canada	12/297	0/0
01/06/2009	Airbus A330-203	F-GZCP	660	near São Pedro, Brazil	12/216	12/216
13/04/2011	Airbus A330-203	F-GZCB	443	Caracas-Simón Bolívar International Airport	13/202	0/0
12/09/2011	Airbus A321-211	F-GTAT	3441	Charles de Gaulle Airport, France	Unknown	0/0
13/12/2011	Airbus A319-111	F-GRHS	1444	Charles de Gaulle Airport, France	5/114	0/0
16/10/2012	Bombardier CRJ-701ER	F-GRZE	10032	Lorient-Lann Bihoué Airport, France	4/53	0/0
11/05/2016	Airbus A320-214	F-GKXJ	1900	Charles de Gaulle Airport, France	5/59	0/0
11/05/2016	Boeing 777-328ER	F-GZNT	38705	Charles de Gaulle Airport, France	1/0	0/0
30/09/2017	Airbus A380-861	F-HPJE	052	over southern Greenland	24/497	0/0
31/10/2018	Airbus A330-203	F-GZCI	502	Charles de Gaulle Airport, France	10/191	0/0
17/06/2022	Boeing 777-228ER	F-GSPQ	28682	New York-John F. Kennedy International Airport, USA	Unknown	0/0

Appendix 2
Air France Fleet Details as of August 2023

Aircraft type	Owned	Leased	On order
Airbus A220-300	6	23	31
Airbus A318-111	4	2	-
Airbus A319-111	11	3	-
Airbus A320-214	2	30	-
Airbus A320-214 sl	3	3	-
Airbus A321-111	4	0	-
Airbus A321-211/212	5	6	-
Airbus A330-203	5	10	-
Airbus A350-941	9	12	4
Airbus A350-941F	0	0	4
Boeing 777-228ER	17	1	-
Boeing 777-328ER	22	21	-
Boeing 777-F28	0	2	-
Boeing 787-9 Dreamliner	7	3	-
Total	**95**	**116**	

Historic Fleet (Including Subsidiary Airlines)

Aircraft type	Total number used	First introduction	Last removed from fleet
Wibault 283 T12	18	1933	1946
Breguet 530 Saigon	2	1934	1936
Latecoere 28-0	1	1933	1935
Latecoere 28-1	20	1933	1937
Latecoere 28-1H	3	1938	1942
Latecoere 28-3	2	1933	1935
Latecoere 300	1	1936	1936
Potez 62	23	1935	1939
Dewoitine D.332	1	1933	1934
Dewoitine D.333	3	1936	1940
Dewoitine D.338	31	1937	1942
Dewoitine D.342	1	1942	1942
Bloch MB.220	16	1937	1948

Aircraft type	Total number used	First introduction	Last removed from fleet
LeO H.213	13	1933	1934
LeO H.242/1	14	1935	1942
LeO H.246.1	7	1939	1947
Farman F224 Centaur II	6	1936	1942
Lockheed 14-H2 Super Electra	1	1940	1943
Lockheed 18-07 Lodestar	5	1940	1945
Lockheed 18-56 Lodestar	1	1942	1942
Latecoere 631	4	1945	1947
SNCASE SE.161 Languedoc	22	1945	1952
SNCASE SE.161/P7 Languedoc	27	1945	1952
Caudron C.444 Goéland	1	1941	1942
Caudron C.445 Goéland	80	1937	1951
Caudron C.447 Goeland	9	1941	1952
Caudron C.448 Goeland	1	1942	1951
Amiot AAC.1 (Junkers Ju-52/3m)	16	1945	1953
de Havilland DH.89A Dragon Rapide	3	1947	1953
de Havilland DH.89B Rapide	1	1947	1952
Douglas DC-3A/B/C/D	83	1946	1962
Douglas DC-4A/-1009	50	1946	1971
Douglas DC-6	2	1956	1969
Lockheed L-049 Constellation	5	1946	1951
Lockheed L-749 Constellation	3	1947	1954
Lockheed L-749A Constellation	20	1947	1964
Lockheed L-749AF Constellation	1	1950	1959
Lockheed L-1049C Super Constellation	9	1950	1976
Lockheed L-1049G Super Constellation	15	1953	1976
Lockheed L-1649A Starliner	9	1957	1967
Breguet 763 Provence	12	1952	1972
De Havilland DH.106 Comet 1A	1	1953	1954
De Havilland DH.106 Comet 1XB	2	1953	1956
North American T-6G Texan	7	1955	1965
North American Harvard MK.IIA	6	1955	1965
Vickers 701 Viscount	2	1967	1968
Vickers 708 Viscount	12	1953	1968
Vickers 739 Viscount	1	1968	1968
Vickers 739A Viscount	1	1968	1968
Sud SE-210 Caravelle III	50	1959	1982
ATR 42-300	8	1986	2013
ATR 42-320	1	1999	2001
ATR 42-500	8	2004	2013
ATR 72-202	1	1999	2005

Air France Fleet Details as of August 2023

Aircraft type	Total number used	First introduction	Last removed from fleet
ATR 72-212	1	2001	2011
ATR 72-212A (500)	7	2006	2013
ATR 72-600	3	2015	2020
Dassault Falcon 20-5	1	1974	1976
Dassault Falcon 20D	1	1974	1976
Hawker Siddeley 748-264 Sr2A	1	1976	1976
Airbus A300B2-1C	11	1974	1997
Airbus A300B4-203	14	1976	1998
Airbus A300B4-2C	2	1976	1999
Airbus A310-203	7	1984	2002
Airbus A310-304	4	1989	2002
Airbus A318-111	12	2006	2023
Airbus A319-111	26	1999	2022
Airbus A319-113	9	1997	2020
Airbus A319-115LR	2	2004	2012
Airbus A320-111	14	1988	2010
Airbus A320-211	43	1989	2017
Airbus A320-212	4	1991	2013
Airbus A320-214	3	2002	2022
Airbus A321-111	1	1997	2022
Airbus A321-211	7	1997	2014
Airbus A321-212	7	1999	2022
Airbus A330-203	1	2005	2009
Airbus A340-211	6	1993	1999
Airbus A340-311	7	1993	2017
Airbus A340-312	1	1993	2005
Airbus A340-313	16	1997	2020
Airbus A380-861	10	2009	2020
Aérospatiale/BAC Concorde	7	1980	2003
Boeing 707-328	21	1959	1978
Boeing 707-328B	8	1962	1983
Boeing 707-328C	11	1965	1982
Boeing 707-355C	1	1968	1981
Boeing 727-228	29	1968	1992
Boeing 737-212(A)	1	1976	1976
Boeing 737-228(A)	17	1982	2002
Boeing 737-222	2	1989	1991
Boeing 737-2K5(A)	2	1998	2001
Boeing 737-247	2	1973	1980
Boeing 737-33A	6	1991	2004
Boeing 737-36N	3	1998	2003

Aircraft type	Total number used	First introduction	Last removed from fleet
Boeing 737-53A	2	1992	2007
Boeing 737-53C	2	1992	1998
Boeing 737-528	14	1991	2007
Boeing 737-5H6	7	1998	2005
Boeing 737-53S	3	1998	2004
Boeing 737-548	2	1999	2005
Boeing 747-121	2	1989	1990
Boeing 747-128	16	1971	2000
Boeing 747-228F	9	1976	2010
Boeing 747-228B	2	1979	2004
Boeing 747-228B(M)	8	1977	2006
Boeing 747-228B(SF)	2	1990	1997
Boeing 747-2B3B(M)(SUD)	2	1992	2006
Boeing 747-2B3F	2	1986	2004
Boeing 747-2D3B(M)	1	1991	1992
Boeing 747-2B4B(M)	2	1989	1991
Boeing 767-27E	2	1999	1999
Boeing 767-3Q8ER	2	1991	2003
Boeing 767-37EER	1	1991	2003
Boeing 767-328ER	4	1993	2003
Boeing 767-33AER	1	1997	1998
Boeing 777-228ER	7	1998	2021
Boeing 777-F28	1	2009	2010
Bombardier CRJ-100ER	13	1997	2013
Bombardier CRJ-200ER	2	2002	2003
Bombardier CRJ-701	15	2001	2013
Bombardier CRJ-900ER	2	2010	2011
Bombardier CRJ-1000EL	12	2011	2013
Bristol 175 Britannia 102	1	1966	1966
British Aerospace 146-100	1	2000	2000
British Aerospace 146-100A	3	2000	2003
British Aerospace 146-200	9	1999	2008
British Aerospace 146-200A	12	1999	2008
British Aerospace 146-200QC	2	2000	2002
British Aerospace 146-300	6	1999	2008
BAE Systems Avro RJ85	15	2006	2014
Convair CV-990-30A-5 Coronado	1	1967	1967
Dornier Do-328-110	5	1997	2000
Douglas DC-8-33F	1	1973	1973
Douglas DC-8-61	1	1990	1990
C-160P Transall	4	1973	1991

Aircraft type	Total number used	First introduction	Last removed from fleet
Embraer EMB-120RT Brasilia	3	1986	1996
Embraer EMB-120ER Brasilia	16	2001	2008
Embraer ERJ-135ER	9	2001	2013
Embraer ERJ-145EP	13	2001	2013
Embraer ERJ-145MP	15	2001	2013
Embraer ERJ-170STD	10	2008	2013
Embraer ERJ-170LR	5	2011	2013
Embraer ERJ-190STD	4	2009	2013
Embraer ERJ-190LR	6	2006	2011
Fokker F27-500 Friendship	13	1968	2003
Fokker F27-500F Friendship	1	1968	2002
Fokker F27-600 Friendship	2	1967	1970
Fokker 70	5	2003	2009
Fokker 100	19	1999	2011
Lockheed L-1011 TriStar 150	1	1989	1991
McDonnell Douglas DC-10-30	5	1992	1995
Saab 340A	4	1987	1995
Saab 340B	1	1989	1991
Saab 2000	7	2001	2006
Beech 1900D	1	2001	2001

Air France Hop Fleet Details at August 2023

Aircraft type	Owned	Leased	On order
Embraer ERJ-170STD	10	0	-
Embraer ERJ-170LR	0	3	-
Embraer ERJ-190STD	4	10	-
Embraer ERJ-190LR	0	6	-

Air France Hop Historic Fleet

Aircraft type	Total number used	First introduction	Last removed from fleet
ATR 72-600 (72-212A)	4	2019	2020
Bombardier CRJ-701	11	2019	2021
Bombardier CRJ-1000EL	14	2019	2022
Embraer ERJ-145EP	7	2019	2020
Embraer ERJ-145MP	6	2019	2020
Embraer ERJ-145LU	1	2019	2020
Embraer ERJ-170LR	2	2019	2022

Other books you might like:

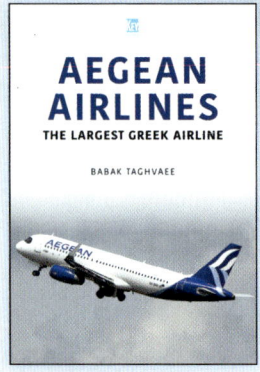
Airlines Series, Vol. 17

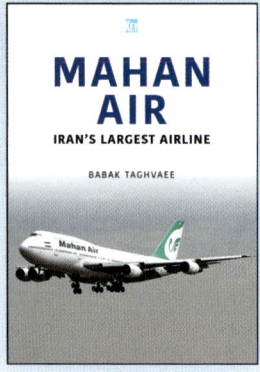
Airlines Series, Vol. 13

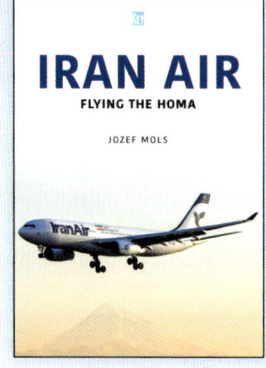
Airlines Series, Vol. 9

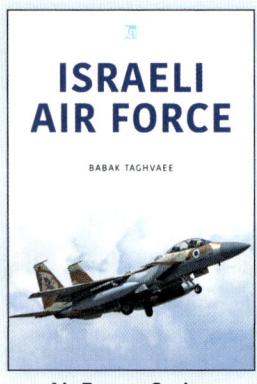
Air Forces Series, Vol. 10

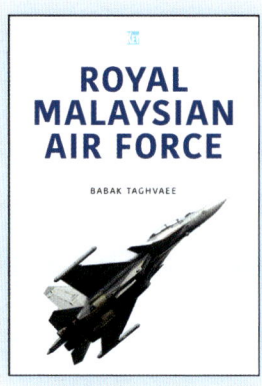
Air Forces Series, Vol. 11

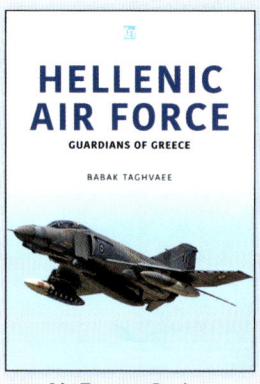
Air Forces Series, Vol. 8

For our full range of titles please visit:
shop.keypublishing.com/books

VIP Book Club

Sign up today and receive
TWO FREE E-BOOKS

Be the first to find out about our forthcoming book releases and receive exclusive offers.

Register now at **keypublishing.com/vip-book-club**

Our VIP Book Club is a 100% spam-free zone, and we will never share your email with anyone else. You can read our full privacy policy at: privacy.keypublishing.com